SMP 11-16

Book Y3

CAMBRIDGE
UNIVERSITY PRESS

Published by the Press Syndicate of the University of Cambridge
The Pitt Building, Trumpington Street, Cambridge CB2 1RP
40 West 20th Street, New York, NY 10011–4211, USA
10 Stamford Road, Oakleigh, Victoria 3166, Australia

© Cambridge University Press 1986

First published 1986
Sixth printing 1992

Illustrations by David Parkins

Cover photograph by Graham Portlock
Diagrams and phototypesetting by Parkway Group, London
and Abingdon, and Gecko Limited, Bicester

Printed in Great Britain at the University Press, Cambridge

British Library cataloguing in publication data
SMP 11–16 yellow series.
  Bk Y3
  1. Mathematics – 1961 –
  I. School Mathematics Project
  510   QA39.2

ISBN 0 521 31479 8

Contents

1	Stretching and enlargement	1
2	Linear relationships	11
	If all you have is . . .	23
3	Vectors	25
	Algebra review (1)	34
4	Percentage (1)	36
5	Mappings	44
6	Investigations (1)	56
	Review 1	57
7	TV programmes survey	61
	If all you have is . . .	67
8	Direct and inverse proportionality	68
9	Representing information	75
	Algebra review (2)	83
10	Looking at data	84
	If all you have is . . .	91
11	Percentage (2)	92
12	Investigations (2)	98
	Algebra review (3)	101
13	Right-angled triangles	102
	Review 2	115
14	Volume	119
15	Problems in planning	124
16	Linear equations	129
17	Distributions	140
	Review 3	152

1 Stretching and enlargement

A

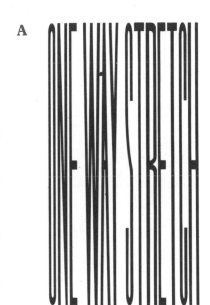

To read the title of this section, hold the bottom of the page close to your eye.

These letters have been drawn by stretching ordinary letters upwards until they are 20 times as tall. The width of each letter has not been altered.

This kind of stretch is called a **one-way stretch**, because the letters were stretched in one direction only.

Here is another one-way stretch. The direction of stretching this time is across. The **stretch factor** is 3.

A shape can be stretched by first drawing it on a grid. The grid is stretched first, and then the stretched shape is drawn on it.

A1 Look at the position of the point marked X on the first drawing. How did the artist know where to mark X′ on the second drawing?

A2 By measuring the grids in the drawings above, find the stretch factor.

A3 Draw a grid and draw a shape of your own on it. Choose a stretch factor, draw a new grid and stretch your shape.

1

A4 Drawing A is stretched to make drawing B.

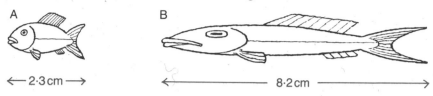

A

B

←2·3 cm→

←————— 8·2 cm —————→

Calculate the stretch factor, to 1 decimal place.

A5 These diagrams show a stretch across with factor 3.

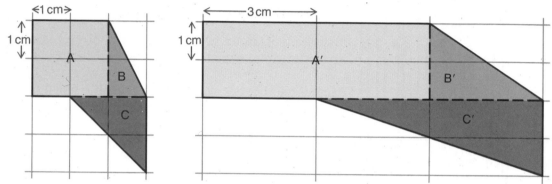

(a) Make a table showing the areas of the marked shapes.

(b) How can you work out the stretched areas from the unstretched areas?

Before stretching	After stretching
A $4\,\text{cm}^2$	A′
B	B′
C	C′
Total	Total

A6 These diagrams show a stretch upwards with factor 2.

(a) Make a table showing the areas of the shapes before and after stretching.

(b) How can you work out the stretched areas from the unstretched areas?

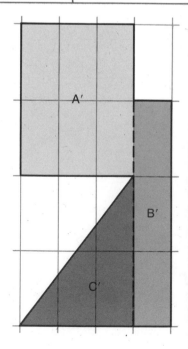

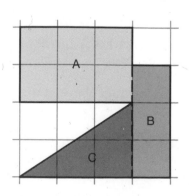

A7 When a square is stretched in the direction of one of its diagonals, we get a rhombus.

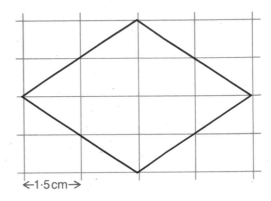

<1 cm>   <1·5cm>

The stretch factor here is 1·5.

(a) Calculate the area of the square.

(b) Calculate the area of the rhombus.

(c) How can you work out the area of the rhombus from that of the square?

A8 In these diagrams a square is stretched upwards with factor 4. The result is a parallelogram.

(a) Calculate the area of the square.

(b) Write down the area of the parallelogram.

(c) If the stretch factor had been 10, what would be the area of the parallelogram?

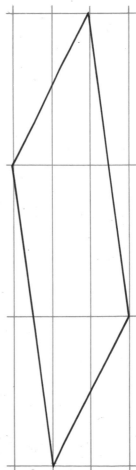

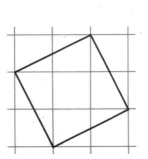

3

When a shape undergoes a one-way stretch, its area is multiplied by
the stretch factor.
You can see why if you think of what happens to a square of area 1 cm².

If you stretch across, with factor 3,
every 1 cm² becomes **3 cm²**.

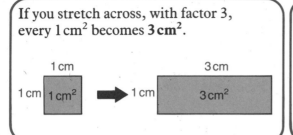

If you stretch up, with factor 2,
every 1 cm² becomes **2 cm²**.

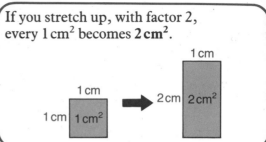

B Stretching a circle

When a circle is given a
one-way stretch, the result
is called an **ellipse**.

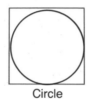

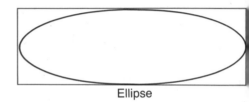

Circle   Ellipse

B1 Follow these instructions for stretching a circle using a
factor of 2.

Draw a circle of radius 2 cm inside a square, and a rectangle 8 cm by 4 cm.

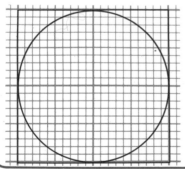

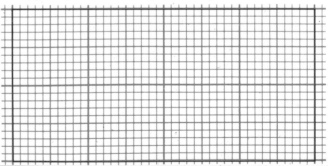

On each line across the square,
measure the distances of the
two points where the circle
crosses the line.

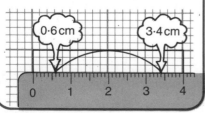

Multiply these distances by the stretch factor 2.
Mark two points inside the rectangle.
When all the points are marked, join them up to
make the ellipse.

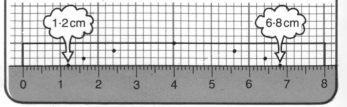

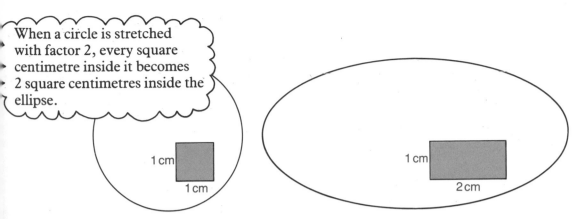

When a circle is stretched with factor 2, every square centimetre inside it becomes 2 square centimetres inside the ellipse.

B2 (a) Use the formula $A = \pi r^2$ to calculate the area of the circle you drew in question B1.

(b) Calculate the area of the ellipse.

B3 (a) What is the stretch factor from this circle to this ellipse?

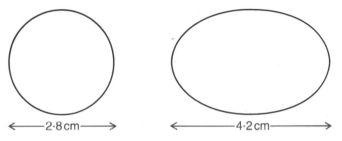

(b) Calculate the area of the circle.

(c) Calculate the area of the ellipse.

B4 Do the same as in question B3 for this circle and ellipse.

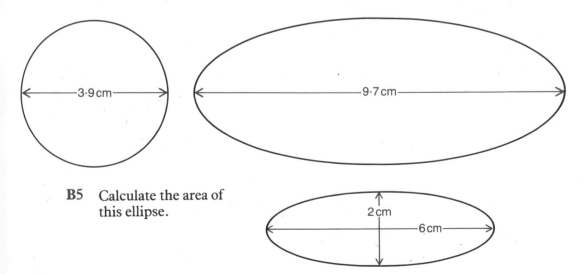

B5 Calculate the area of this ellipse.

5

c Two-way stretches

These diagrams show a **two-way stretch**.

The left-hand shape has been stretched
across by a factor of 2 and up by a
factor of 3.

C1 (a) Calculate the area of
each part before and
after the two-way stretch.

   (b) What do you multiply
the unstretched area by
to get the stretched area?

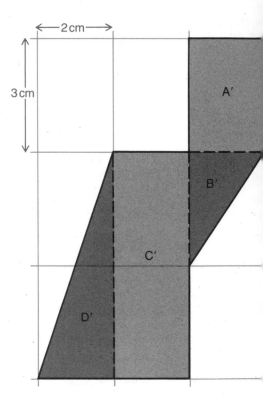

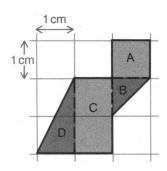

When a shape undergoes a two-way stretch, its area is multiplied
by **both** stretch factors.

Once again, you can see why by thinking of what happens to
every $1\,\text{cm}^2$.

If you stretch across with factor 2
and up with factor 3, every $1\,\text{cm}^2$
becomes $(2 \times 3)\,\text{cm}^2$.

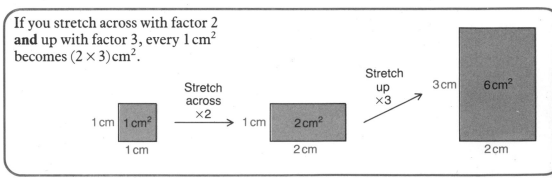

C2 (a) What is the area of this shape?

   (b) What will the area be after a
two-way stretch, across with
factor 5 and up with factor 4?

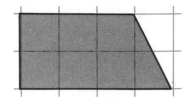

C3 A shape whose area is 4·5 cm² is given a two-way stretch, across with factor 4 and up with factor 3·5.
What is its area after the two-way stretch?

C4 When a circle is given a two-way stretch, the result is an ellipse.

This is what you get when you stretch a circle of radius 1 cm across with factor 2·5 and up with factor 1·5.

(a) Calculate the area of the circle.

(b) Calculate the area of the ellipse.

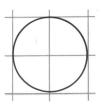 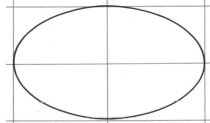

C5 A circle of radius 1 cm was given a two-way stretch, across and up. The result was this ellipse.

(a) Measure the ellipse to find the stretch factors, across and up.

(b) Calculate the area of the ellipse.

Anamorphic film

If you look at this piece of film you will see that the picture is 'squashed'. The film is shown on a wide screen. A special lens in the projector stretches the picture horizontally more than it stretches it vertically, so that the picture looks right on the wide screen.

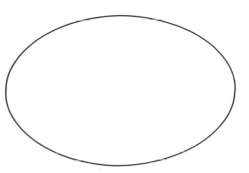

The camera which is used to make the film has a special lens which squashes the picture horizontally to fit the frame of the film. In this way ordinary film can be used to make pictures for the wide screen.

A detail from the frame above

D Enlargement and reduction

Here is a two-way stretch in which both factors are 3.

This kind of two-way stretch, where both factors are equal, is an **enlargement**.

3 is the **scale factor** of the enlargement shown here.

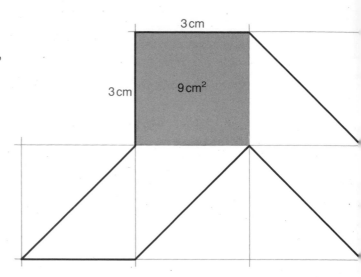

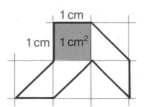

The 3 times enlargement can be thought of as a two-way stretch, with factors 3 across and 3 up.

The stretch across multiplies areas by 3.
The stretch up multiplies them by 3 again.

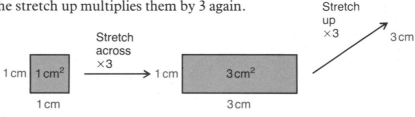

So altogether the area is multiplied by 3×3 or 3^2.

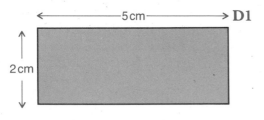

D1 (a) This rectangle is to be enlarged by a scale factor of 4. Calculate the length and the height of the enlarged rectangle.
(b) Calculate the area of the rectangle before, and after, the enlargement.
(c) What is the area multiplied by when the rectangle is enlarged by a scale factor of 4?

D2 Re-do question D1, but with an enlargement with scale factor 5.

D3 What is the area multiplied by if the scale factor of an enlargement is (a) 6 (b) 10 (c) 2 (d) 8 (e) 7

D4 A shape whose area is $8\,cm^2$ is enlarged with a scale factor of 5. What is the new area?

Let k stand for the scale factor of an enlargement. If a shape is enlarged by a scale factor k, then its area is multiplied by k^2.

We say the **area factor** of the enlargement is k^2.

D5 What is the area factor of an enlargement whose scale factor is

(a) 5   (b) 9   (c) 2·5   (d) 3·5   (e) 1·732

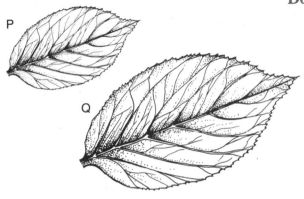

D6 Shape Q is an enlargement of shape P.

(a) Measure the length of each shape. From these measurements calculate the scale factor of the enlargement, to 1 d.p.

(b) Calculate the area factor of the enlargement.

(c) If the area of P is 3·8 cm^2, what is the area of Q (to the nearest 0·1 cm^2)?

*D7 If you want to enlarge a photo so that its area is doubled, what scale factor do you use for the enlargement?

When the scale factor is less than 1, instead of an enlargement we have a **reduction**.
(Often the word 'enlargement' is used to cover reductions as well.)

In this diagram, shape A undergoes a reduction and the result is shape B.
The scale factor is 0·8.

A square 1 cm by 1 cm in shape A becomes a square 0·8 cm by 0·8 cm in B.

So 1 cm^2 in A becomes 0·64 cm^2 in B.

The area factor of the reduction is **0·8^2** or **0·64**.

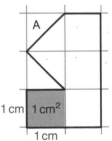

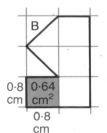

The rule **area factor = (scale factor)^2** applies to reductions as well.

D8 (a) What is the area of shape A?

(b) What is the area of shape B?

D9 What is the area factor of a reduction whose scale factor is

(a) $\frac{1}{2}$ (b) $\frac{1}{3}$ (c) 0·4   (d) 0·3   (e) 0·1

D10 On a map of England, the county of Essex covers an area, on the map, of $18{\cdot}4\,\text{cm}^2$.
The map undergoes a reduction with scale factor $0{\cdot}6$.
Calculate the area covered by Essex on the reduced map.

A

D11 Picture B is a reduction of picture A.

B

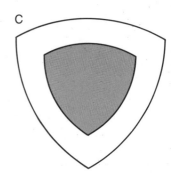

(a) Measure the length of each picture. Work out the scale factor of the reduction from your measurements, to 1 d.p.

(b) If the area of A is $5{\cdot}4\,\text{cm}^2$, calculate the area of B.

D12 (a) Look at these three 'shields'. In which of them do you think half the area is shaded? Decide without measuring. Write down your answer.

A

B

C

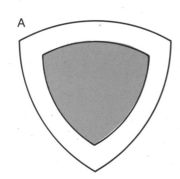
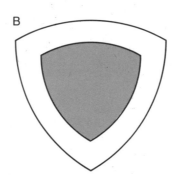

(b) Estimate what fraction of the area is shaded in each of the other two shields.

(c) In each case the outline of the shaded part is a reduction of the outline of the shield. Measure the widths of the shield and of the shaded part and work out the scale factor of each reduction.

(d) Calculate the area factor of each reduction. Compare the results with the answers you got by estimating.

*D13 If you want to reduce a photo so that its area is $\frac{1}{10}$ of what it was before, what scale factor do you use?

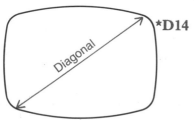

Diagonal

*D14 The size of a TV screen is usually stated by giving the length of a diagonal of the screen.

If a '20-inch' screen has an area of $1250\,\text{cm}^2$, what is the area of
(a) a 16-inch screen   (b) a 12-inch screen
(c) a 22-inch screen   (d) a 24-inch screen

10

2 Linear relationships

A Gradients of lines

The diagram on the right shows what we mean
by the **gradient** of a line.

A and B are any two points on the line.
The distance **across** from A to B is a.
The distance **up** from A to B is u.

The gradient of the line is the ratio $\frac{u}{a}$.

This ratio is the same no matter which two
points on the line are chosen as A and B.

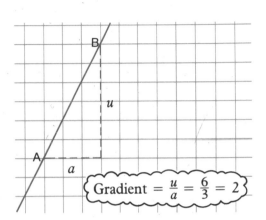

Gradient $= \frac{u}{a} = \frac{6}{3} = 2$

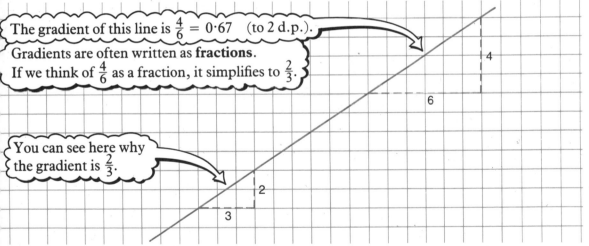

The gradient of this line is $\frac{4}{6} = 0 \cdot 67$ (to 2 d.p.).

Gradients are often written as **fractions**.
If we think of $\frac{4}{6}$ as a fraction, it simplifies to $\frac{2}{3}$.

You can see here why
the gradient is $\frac{2}{3}$.

A1 Write down the gradient of each of these lines, as a
fraction or a whole number.

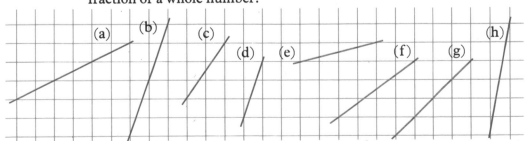

(a) (b) (c) (d) (e) (f) (g) (h)

A2 Which two lines in question A1 have the same gradient?
What can you say about these two lines?

A3 What is the gradient of the line from $(1, 2)$ to $(6, 5)$? (See the diagram on the right.)

A4 What is the gradient of the line from
(a) $(0, 0)$ to $(3, 5)$ (b) $(0, 0)$ to $(6, 3)$
(c) $(1, 1)$ to $(5, 3)$ (d) $(2, 3)$ to $(7, 11)$
(e) $(0, 2)$ to $(10, 6)$ (f) $(16, 7)$ to $(20, 19)$

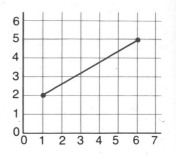

B Positive and negative gradients

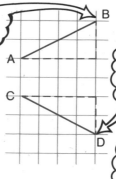

From A to B is 4 **across** and 2 **up**.
So the gradient of AB is $\frac{2}{4} = \frac{1}{2} = 0 \cdot 5$.

From C to D is also 4 across, but then you go 2 **down** instead of 2 up.

So you put ⁻2 instead of 2 when you work out the gradient of CD.

Gradient $= \frac{^-2}{4} = \frac{^-1}{2} = ^-0 \cdot 5$

Lines which slope **downwards** from left to right have **negative** gradients. (We always measure across from left to right.)

B1 Write down the gradient of each of these lines.

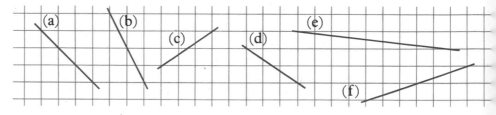

B2 What is the gradient of the line through
(a) $(1, 5)$ and $(5, 3)$ (See diagram.)
(b) $(0, 6)$ and $(2, 0)$
(c) $(3, 0)$ and $(5, 5)$
(d) $(4, 7)$ and $(7, 4)$
(e) $(1, 2)$ and $(8, 1)$

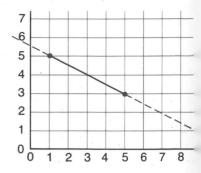

If you are given the coordinates of two points, you can find
the gradient of the line through them like this.

1 Suppose the points are $(^-2, 3)$ and $(4, ^-1)$. Draw a rough sketch to show their positions.

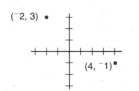

2 Draw the line through them. Mark the distances you will need for working out the gradient.

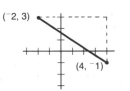

3 Work out the distances across and up (or down) from the coordinates.

From $^-2$ to 4 is 6.

From 3 to $^-1$ is $^-4$.

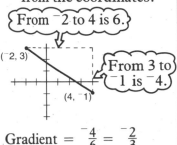

$$\text{Gradient} = \frac{^-4}{6} = \frac{^-2}{3}$$

B3 Find the gradient of the line through
   (a) $(1, 2)$ and $(3, 3)$ (b) $(1, 4)$ and $(4, 1)$ (c) $(^-1, ^-3)$ and $(2, 4)$
   (d) $(^-4, 2)$ and $(3, 0)$ (e) $(5, 3)$ and $(^-2, ^-3)$ (f) $(^-3, 4)$ and $(1, ^-2)$

B4 The lines AB and AC in this diagram are at right-angles. So are PQ and PR, and also XY and XZ.

   (a) Write down the gradient of

     (i) AB   (ii) AC

     (iii) PQ   (iv) PR

     (v) XY   (vi) XZ

   (b) What is the rule connecting the gradients of two lines at right-angles to each other?

   (c) Write down the gradient of a line at right-angles to another line whose gradient is $\frac{^-3}{4}$.

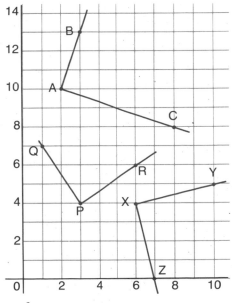

B5 Here are the gradients of eight lines *a* to *h*.

Line	*a*	*b*	*c*	*d*	*e*	*f*	*g*	*h*
Gradient	$^-\frac{1}{5}$	5	$\frac{1}{5}$	$\frac{2}{5}$	$^-5$	5	$\frac{1}{5}$	$^-2\frac{1}{2}$

   (a) Which lines are parallel to each other?
   (b) Which pairs of lines are at right-angles to each other?

B6 What would you say about the gradient of a line parallel to the *y*-axis?

C Gradient and intercept

A do-it-yourself shop charges £2 per metre for planed timber of a certain width and thickness.

Let l be the length in metres of a piece of timber, and let C be its cost in £.

This table shows some pairs of values of l and C.

Length in m	l	0	1	2	3	4
Cost in £	C	0	2	4	6	8

C and l are connected by the formula $C = 2l$.

The graph of (l, C) is shown on the right.
Its gradient is **2**.

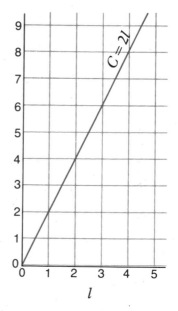

Now suppose the shop charges an extra £3 for delivering the timber, regardless of the amount bought.

If C now stands for the total cost of the timber plus the delivery charge, the table looks like this.

Length in m	l	0	1	2	3	4
Timber cost in £		0	2	4	6	8
Delivery in £		3	3	3	3	3
Total cost in £	C	3	5	7	9	11

The effect on the graph of the additional charge of £3 is to move every point **3 units up**.

The formula is now $C = 2l + 3$ instead of $C = 2l$.

The graph still has a gradient of **2**.
It is parallel to the first graph.

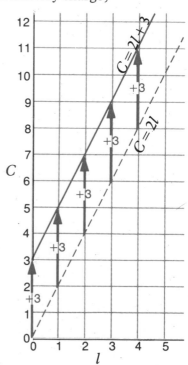

Look at the point at $(0, 0)$ on the graph of $C = 2l$.

This point moves up to $(0, 3)$ on the graph of $C = 2l + 3$.

The number 3 is called the **intercept** of the graph of $C = 2l + 3$ on the C-axis.

Intercept

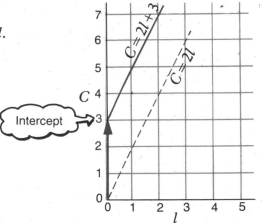

C1 The shop charges £3 per metre for timber of a different kind.

(a) If there is no delivery charge, what is the formula connecting C and l in this case?

(b) Draw the graph of (l, C) for this formula.

(c) If the delivery charge is £2, what is the formula connecting C and l when the delivery charge is included?

(d) Draw the graph for this formula on the same axes.

(e) What is the gradient of the first graph?

(f) What is the gradient of the second graph?

(g) What is the intercept of the second graph on the C-axis?

C2 The formula for the cost, including a delivery charge, of a different kind of wood is $C = 5l + 4$.

(a) What is the cost per metre of the wood?

(b) What is the delivery charge?

(c) What is the gradient of the graph of $C = 5l + 4$?

(d) What is its intercept on the C-axis?

C3 Draw x- and y-axes with x and y both from 0 to 10.

(a) Copy and complete this table for the formula $y = \frac{1}{2}x$.

x	0	2	4	6	8	10
y						

(b) Draw and label the graph of $y = \frac{1}{2}x$.

(c) Copy and complete a similar table for $y = \frac{1}{2}x + 3$.

(d) Draw and label the graph of $y = \frac{1}{2}x + 3$.

(e) What is the gradient of the graph of $y = \frac{1}{2}x + 3$?

(f) What is its intercept on the y-axis?

15

C4 (a) Copy and complete this table for the formula $y = 2x - 3$.

x	0	1	2	3	4	5
y	$^-3$					

(b) Draw the graph of $y = 2x - 3$.

(c) What is the gradient of the graph?

(d) What is its intercept on the y-axis?

C5 Without drawing graphs write down (i) the gradient, (ii) the intercept on the y-axis, of each of these graphs.

(a) $y = 3x + 4$ (b) $y = 7x + 2$ (c) $y = 7x - 2$ (d) $y = \frac{1}{3}x - 4$

(e) $y = x + 3$ (f) $y = 6x - 6$ (g) $y = 5 + 4x$ (h) $y = {}^-4 + 2x$

C6 In the diagram on the right, the line through $(0, 0)$ has the equation $y = 1 \cdot 5x$.

The other lines are all parallel to it. Write down the equation of each one.

C7 In the diagram below,

(a) What is the gradient of line a?

(b) Write down the equation of line a.

(c) Write down the equation of line b.

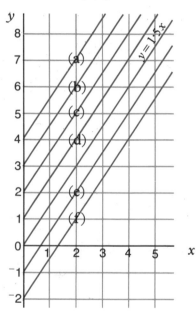

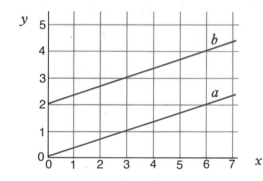

C8 In the diagram on the right,

(a) What is the gradient of line p?

(b) What is its intercept on the y-axis?

(c) Write down the equation of line p.

(d) Write down the equation of line q.

(e) Write down the equation of line r.

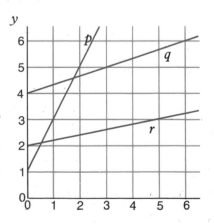

D Lines with negative gradients

The equation $y = {}^-2x$ gives this table of values.

x	0	1	2	3	4	5
y	0	$^-2$	$^-4$	$^-6$	$^-8$	$^-10$

When x is 3, $y = {}^-2 \times 3 = {}^-6$.

The graph of $y = {}^-2x$ looks like this.

The gradient is $^-2$.

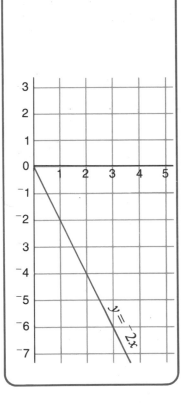

Change the equation to $y = {}^-2x + 3$.
The line $y = {}^-2x$ moves 3 units upwards.

The gradient is still $^-2$.
The intercept on the y-axis is 3.

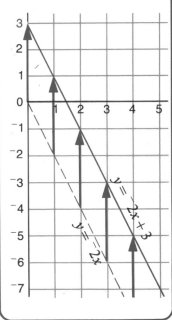

Change the equation to $y = {}^-2x - 3$.
The line $y = {}^-2x$ moves 3 units downwards.

The gradient is still $^-2$.
The intercept on the y-axis is $^-3$.

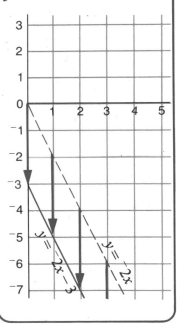

D1 (a) Copy and complete this table for the equation $y = {}^-\frac{1}{2}x$.

x	0	2	4	6	8	10
y						

(b) Draw axes with x from 0 to 10 and y from $^-5$ to 5.
Draw and label the graph of $y = {}^-\frac{1}{2}x$.

(c) Make a similar table of values for $y = {}^-\frac{1}{2}x + 4$.

(d) On the same axes draw and label the graph of $y = {}^-\frac{1}{2}x + 4$.

(e) What is (i) the gradient, (ii) the intercept on the y-axis, of $y = {}^-\frac{1}{2}x + 4$?

D2 Without drawing, write down (i) the gradient, (ii) the intercept on the y-axis, of each of these graphs.

(a) $y = {}^-5x + 1$ (b) $y = {}^-5x - 2$ (c) $y = 0.1x - 3.8$ (d) $y = {}^-4x + 7$

D3 In the diagram on the right, the line through (0, 0) has the equation $y = {}^-\frac{1}{2}x$.

The other lines are parallel to it. Write down the equation of each one.

D4 In the diagram below,

(a) What is the gradient of line *a*?

(b) What is the gradient of line *b*?

(c) Write down the equation of line *b*.

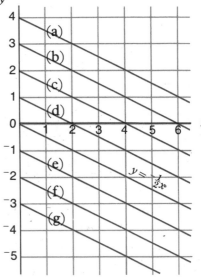

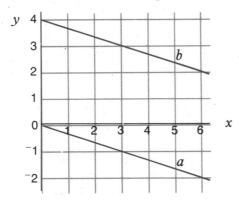

D5 In the diagram on the right,

(a)   (i). What is the gradient of line *a*?
     (ii) What is its intercept on the y-axis?
     (iii) Write down the equation of line *a*.

(b) Write down the equation of line *b*.

(c) Write down the equation of line *c*.

(d) Write down the equation of line *d*.

(e) Write down the equation of line *e*.

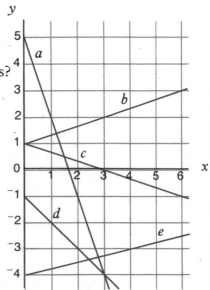

18

E Fitting a linear formula

Two students were looking over an old warehouse which was going to be demolished. They found a rope and pulleys which had been used for lifting sacks.

They decided to investigate the relationship between the load being lifted up and the amount of pull needed on the free end of the rope. They hung various loads on the hook; each time they found out how much weight on the free end would just balance the load.

Here are the measurements they got. L stands for the load in kg, and B for the balancing weight in kg.

L	5·0	8·0	9·0	12·0
B	4·9	6·4	6·9	8·4

They could not see any relationship between L and B, so they drew a graph. The four points were all in a straight line.

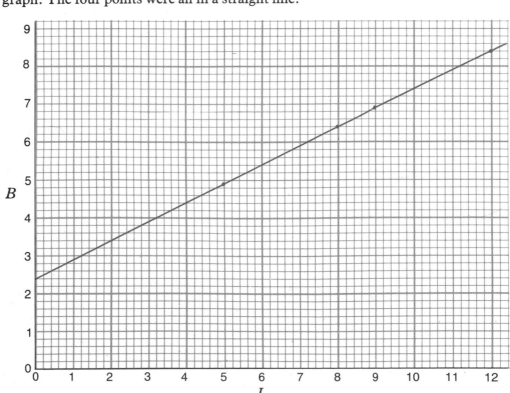

E1 (a) Choose any two points on the graph and use them to find the gradient of the line.
   (b) What is the intercept on the B-axis?
   (c) Write down the equation of the line in the form $B = \ldots L + \ldots$
   (d) Check that the numbers in the table fit the equation.

E2 The table below shows the load L, in tonnes, which can be supported on a certain type of girder when the thickness of the girder is t cm.

t	10	30	50	60
L	120	290	460	545

(a) Plot the four pairs of values on the graph paper. Suitable scales are shown here. Draw the line through the points.

(b) Find the gradient of the line by choosing two points on it (the further apart the better). When you measure across and up, you must use the scales on the axes. (Across, 1 small square is 1, up it is 10.) Write the gradient as a **decimal**.

(c) Write down the intercept of the line on the L-axis.

(d) Write down the equation of the line.

(e) Check that the equation fits all the numbers in the table.

In the last example and the previous one, the points plotted were all exactly on a straight line. In practice this does not happen with real measurements.

When the points are quite close to being on a straight line you can draw a 'line of best fit'. You do this by eye: some points will be above your line and some below.

You can find the equation of your line by the usual 'gradient and intercept' method. Use **decimals**.

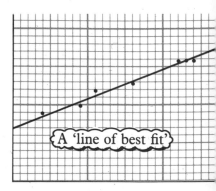

A 'line of best fit'

E3 A weighing machine was being checked for accuracy. In the table below I stands for the weight, in kg, indicated by the machine and W stands for the true weight, in kg, placed on the machine.

I	10	20	30	40	50
W	15	22	31	37	45

(a) Plot the values of (I, W) on graph paper.

(b) Draw a line of best fit.

(c) Find the gradient and intercept (use decimals) and write the equation of the line.

E4 When some gas is sealed in a container and heated, the pressure of the gas increases as the temperature increases.

Here are some measurements of the température t, in °C, and the pressure p, in millibars, of the gas in a sealed container.

t	15	65	100	180	250
p	1500	1750	1950	2350	2700

(a) Plot the values of (t, p) and draw a line of best fit.
(Suitable scales are: for t, 1 cm to 25; for p, 1 cm to 250.)

(b) Find the equation of the line.

(c) Use your equation to predict what p will be when t is 400.

(d) The maximum pressure which the container can withstand is 6000 millibars. Use your equation to calculate a value for the maximum temperature to which the container can be heated.

E5 Diana's car has a faulty speedometer. When it was checked, these were the results.

I (indicated speed in m.p.h.)	20	30	40	50	60
T (true speed in m.p.h.)	19	29	44	54	67

(a) Draw axes with I from 0 to 60 and T from $^-$10 to 70.
Plot the values of (I, T) and draw a line of best fit.

(b) Find the equation of your line.

(c) According to the straight-line graph, when the speedometer indicates 0 m.p.h. the true speed is negative, so the car would be going backwards! This is not likely to be true! It is more likely that the pointer on the speedometer 'sticks' at a certain lowest value. Read from your graph what that value is.

F Re-arranging equations into gradient–intercept form

The graph of $y = 3x + 5$ is a straight line with gradient 3, whose intercept on the y-axis is 5.
In general we can say that the graph of $y = ax + b$ is a straight line with gradient a, whose intercept on the y-axis is b.

Sometimes an equation is not written in the form $y = ax + b$, but can be re-arranged into this form. We can then find the gradient and intercept.

For example, $y = 5 + 2x$ can be re-written $y = 2x + 5$, so a is 2 and b is 5.
$\qquad y = 3 - 4x$ can be re-written $y = 3 + {}^-4x$
$\qquad\qquad\qquad\qquad$ or $y = {}^-4x + 3$, so a is $^-4$ and b is 3.

F1 Re-write these equations in the form $y = ax + b$.
(a) $y = 7 + 4x$ (b) $y = {}^-2 + 3x$ (c) $y = 6 - x$ (d) $y = 5 - 6x$

When an equation is written in the form $y = ax + b$, we say it is
in **gradient–intercept** form.

Sometimes it is not so easy to re-arrange an equation into
gradient–intercept form. Here are some examples.

Worked examples

(1) Re-write the equation $2x + y = 10$ in gradient–intercept form.

We must re-write the equation in the form $y = \ldots$

$$2x + y = 10$$

Subtract $2x$ from both sides. $\quad y = 10 - 2x$

Re-write in the form $y = ax + b$. $\quad \mathbf{y = {}^-2x + 10}$

(2) Re-write the equation $2x + 5y = 4$ in gradient–intercept form.

$$2x + 5y = 4$$

Subtract $2x$ from both sides. $\quad 5y = 4 - 2x$

Divide both sides by 5. $\quad y = \dfrac{4 - 2x}{5}$

See the bottom of the page for
the explanation of this step. $\quad y = \dfrac{4}{5} - \dfrac{2x}{5}$

Re-write in the form $y = ax + b$. $\quad y = {}^-\tfrac{2}{5}x + \tfrac{4}{5}$

F2 Re-write each of these equations in gradient–intercept form,
and write down the gradient in each case.

(a) $3x + y = 4$ (b) $y - 4x = 6$ (c) $y + 2x = 10$

(d) $x + 3y = 12$ (e) $3x + 4y = 8$ (f) $x - y = 7$

(g) $x - 2y = 9$ (h) $4y - x = 5$ (i) $2x - 3y = 15$

(j) $3 - y = x$ (k) $3y - 1 = 5x$ (l) $4x - 3y = 10$

$\dfrac{\text{Something}}{5}$ is the same as $\dfrac{1}{5}(\text{something})$

So $\dfrac{4 - 2x}{5} = \dfrac{1}{5}(4 - 2x) = \dfrac{1}{5} \times 4 - \dfrac{1}{5} \times 2x = \dfrac{4}{5} - \dfrac{2x}{5}$.

If all you have is ...

a pencil,
a pair of compasses,
and a straight edge,

you can draw an angle of 60° like this.

Set the compasses to any radius. Draw an arc (part of a circle).	Don't alter the radius. Put the compasses point somewhere on the arc. Draw another arc.	Use the straight edge to draw these two lines. The angle between them is 60°.
Centre •	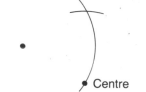 • Centre	

The reason why the angle must be 60° is because it is one of the angles of an equilateral triangle.

This is an example of a geometrical **construction**. A construction is a drawing task which has to be carried out using only the instruments you are told you can use. There must be no guesswork, or estimating things 'by eye'.

Here is another construction using the same instruments. Follow the instructions yourself.

How to divide a given angle exactly in half

Set the compasses to any radius. Put the point at the vertex O of the angle. Draw arcs to cut the arms of the angle.	Set the compasses to any radius greater than half the distance PQ. Put the point at P and draw an arc, then at Q.	Use the straight edge to join O to R. The line OR cuts the angle POQ in half.
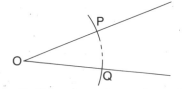 Let P, Q be the points where the arcs cross the arms.	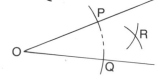 Let R be the point where the two arcs cross.	

Can you explain why the line OR must divide the angle POQ exactly in half?

Dividing an angle in half is also called 'bisecting' it.

1 Use the construction for bisecting an angle to

(a) bisect an angle of 180° into two right-angles

(b) bisect one of the right-angles into two angles of 45°

2 Show how to construct an angle of 30° using only a pencil, compasses and a straight edge.
For a 'straight edge' you can use one edge of a ruler, but you must take no notice of the measurements marked on it.

3 Show how to construct a square using only a pencil, compasses and a straight edge.

4 Draw a triangle of any shape.
Bisect each of the three angles.

What do you notice about the three lines which bisect the angles?

5 Draw two lines intersecting at a point. They form an 'X' shape.

Bisect each of the four angles made by the two lines.

What do you notice about the lines which bisect the angles?

Can you explain why it is?

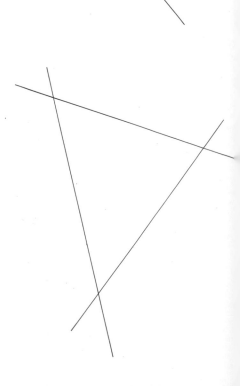

6 When the sides of a triangle are extended, an 'X' is formed at each corner of the triangle.

Draw a triangle. Extend its sides. Construct the lines which bisect the angles at each X, as in question 5.

If you do it accurately, you will find that the lines you draw will meet three at a time at various points.

3 Vectors

A Displacement vectors

A helicopter sets out from the point A on this map, and travels in a straight line to a point B.

The distance from A to B is 20 km.

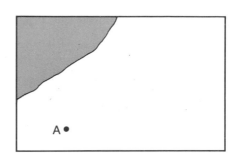

If we want to mark B, the information given is not enough. We need to know the **direction** in which the helicopter travelled.

The usual way of giving the direction of a line on a map is to give its **bearing**.

A line pointing north has a bearing of 0°. All other bearings are measured from north, **clockwise**.

Bearings are usually written as 3-figure numbers.

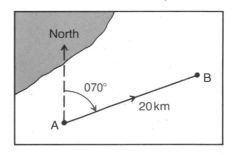

If we are told that the helicopter travelled 20 km on a bearing 070°, we can mark B on the map.

The line going from A to B in the direction of the arrow is called a **displacement vector**. (In this chapter we shall use the word **vector** by itself to mean 'displacement vector'.)

The symbol for the vector from A to B is $\overrightarrow{AB}$.

We can describe the vector $\overrightarrow{AB}$ completely by giving its **length** (20 km) and its **direction** (bearing 070°).

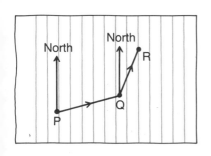

A1 Turn your page round so that the lines go up the page. Use the upward direction as north.

(a) Mark a point P on your page. An aircraft travels from P along the vector $\overrightarrow{PQ}$ (50 km, bearing 075°). Draw the vector $\overrightarrow{PQ}$ to scale, using 1 cm to stand for 10 km.

(b) From Q the aircraft travels along $\overrightarrow{QR}$ (40 km, bearing 020°). Draw a line at Q pointing north, measure the angle of 20° and draw $\overrightarrow{QR}$ to scale.

(c) Measure the length and bearing of the vector $\overrightarrow{PR}$.

Turn your page round as in question A1 for questions A2 to A5.

A2 A motorboat starts at a point A and travels along the vector
$\overrightarrow{AB}$ (35 km, bearing 030°). From B it travels along the vector
$\overrightarrow{BC}$ (45 km, bearing 110°).

Draw the vectors $\overrightarrow{AB}$ and $\overrightarrow{BC}$ to scale, and measure the length
and bearing of the vector $\overrightarrow{AC}$.

A3 A yacht sails from X to Y, then from Y to Z.

$\overrightarrow{XY}$ is 55 km on a bearing 100°. $\overrightarrow{YZ}$ is 25 km on a bearing 200°.

Find from a scale drawing the length and bearing of the vector $\overrightarrow{XZ}$.

If A and B are two points, then the vectors $\overrightarrow{AB}$ and $\overrightarrow{BA}$ are in opposite
directions and have **different** bearings.

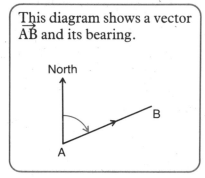

This diagram shows a vector $\overrightarrow{AB}$ and its bearing.

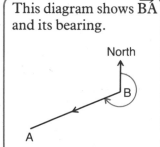

This diagram shows $\overrightarrow{BA}$ and its bearing.

The bearing is measured at the **starting point** of the vector.

A4 A yacht sails on a triangular course ABC.

$\overrightarrow{AB}$ is 40 km on a bearing 145°. $\overrightarrow{BC}$ is 50 km on a bearing 250°.

Find from a scale drawing the length and bearing of $\overrightarrow{CA}$.

A5 A light aircraft flies on a triangular course PQR.

$\overrightarrow{PQ}$ is 32 km on a bearing 295°. $\overrightarrow{QR}$ is 57 km on a bearing 080°.

Find from a scale drawing the length and bearing of $\overrightarrow{RP}$.

*A6 (a) If the bearing of $\overrightarrow{AB}$ is 070°
 calculate the bearing of $\overrightarrow{BA}$.

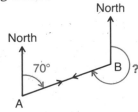

(b) Draw a sketch of a vector $\overrightarrow{AB}$
 whose bearing is 130°, and
 calculate the bearing of $\overrightarrow{BA}$.

(c) Repeat part (b) for when the bearing of $\overrightarrow{AB}$ is   (i) 200°   (ii) 300°

(d) Can you find any rules for working out the bearing of $\overrightarrow{BA}$ when
 you are told the bearing of $\overrightarrow{AB}$?

26

B   Column vectors

If the points A and B are on a grid of squares, we can describe the vector $\vec{AB}$ by using two numbers.

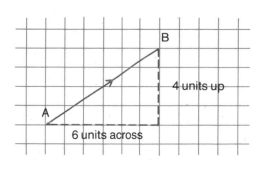

The number of units **across**:   6

The number of units **up**:   4

We write the two numbers one above the other, in square brackets.

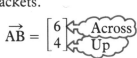

$$\vec{AB} = \begin{bmatrix} 6 \\ 4 \end{bmatrix}$$

$\begin{bmatrix} 6 \\ 4 \end{bmatrix}$ is called a **column vector**. (The two numbers are written in a column.)

As with coordinates, we have to distinguish between **positive** and **negative**.

Across to the **right** is **positive** and to the **left** is **negative**.

Upwards is **positive**, and **downwards** is **negative**.

Here are some examples of column vectors with positive and negative numbers.

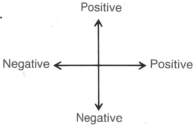

$\begin{bmatrix} 3 \\ -4 \end{bmatrix}$ means   3 to the **right** 4 **down**

$\begin{bmatrix} -3 \\ 2 \end{bmatrix}$ means   3 to the **left** 2 **up**

$\begin{bmatrix} -5 \\ -2 \end{bmatrix}$ means   5 to the **left** 2 **down**

$\begin{bmatrix} 2 \\ 4 \end{bmatrix}$ means   2 to the **right** 4 **up**

B1   Write down the column vector of each of these vectors.

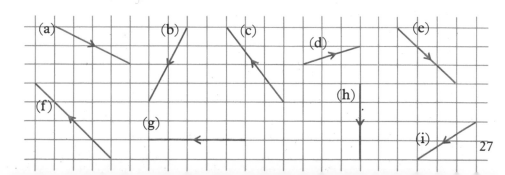

27

B2 On squared paper draw vectors which have these column vectors.

(a) $\begin{bmatrix} 3 \\ 5 \end{bmatrix}$ (b) $\begin{bmatrix} 5 \\ 3 \end{bmatrix}$ (c) $\begin{bmatrix} 5 \\ -3 \end{bmatrix}$ (d) $\begin{bmatrix} -3 \\ -5 \end{bmatrix}$ (e) $\begin{bmatrix} -5 \\ 3 \end{bmatrix}$

When two vectors have the same column vector, we say they are **equal** to each other.

In this diagram, $\overrightarrow{AB} = \overrightarrow{CD}$ because both of them are equal to $\begin{bmatrix} 5 \\ 2 \end{bmatrix}$.

But $\overrightarrow{AB}$ is **not** equal to $\overrightarrow{EF}$, because the column vector of $\overrightarrow{EF}$ is $\begin{bmatrix} 5 \\ -2 \end{bmatrix}$.

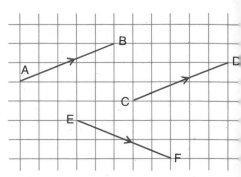

B3 Which vectors in this diagram are equal to one another?

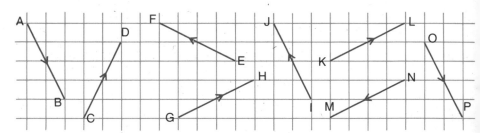

The vector from A to B in this diagram is $\begin{bmatrix} 3 \\ -4 \end{bmatrix}$.

The vector which takes you back from B to A is $\begin{bmatrix} -3 \\ 4 \end{bmatrix}$.

$\begin{bmatrix} -3 \\ 4 \end{bmatrix}$ is called the **inverse** of $\begin{bmatrix} 3 \\ -4 \end{bmatrix}$.

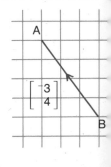

B4 Write down the inverse of each of these vectors.
(Draw diagrams if it helps you.)

(a) $\begin{bmatrix} 4 \\ 5 \end{bmatrix}$ (b) $\begin{bmatrix} -1 \\ 4 \end{bmatrix}$ (c) $\begin{bmatrix} 5 \\ -2 \end{bmatrix}$ (d) $\begin{bmatrix} -3 \\ -4 \end{bmatrix}$ (e) $\begin{bmatrix} 2 \\ 0 \end{bmatrix}$

(f) $\begin{bmatrix} 0 \\ -5 \end{bmatrix}$ (g) $\begin{bmatrix} 0 \\ 7 \end{bmatrix}$ (h) $\begin{bmatrix} -6 \\ 0 \end{bmatrix}$ (i) $\begin{bmatrix} 6 \\ -7 \end{bmatrix}$ (j) $\begin{bmatrix} -2 \\ 8 \end{bmatrix}$

C Adding vectors

In this diagram, $\vec{AB} = \begin{bmatrix} 5 \\ 2 \end{bmatrix}$ and $\vec{BC} = \begin{bmatrix} 3 \\ 4 \end{bmatrix}$.

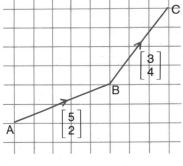

We can add the two vectors together, like this.

$$\begin{bmatrix} 5 \\ 2 \end{bmatrix} + \begin{bmatrix} 3 \\ 4 \end{bmatrix} = \begin{bmatrix} 8 \\ 6 \end{bmatrix}$$

The top numbers add up to 8.

The bottom numbers add up to 6.

The result, $\begin{bmatrix} 8 \\ 6 \end{bmatrix}$, is the column vector of $\vec{AC}$.

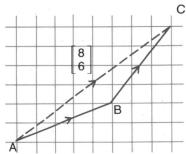

$$\begin{array}{ccc} \vec{AB} & \vec{BC} & \vec{AC} \\ \begin{bmatrix} 5 \\ 2 \end{bmatrix} + \begin{bmatrix} 3 \\ 4 \end{bmatrix} & = & \begin{bmatrix} 8 \\ 6 \end{bmatrix} \end{array}$$

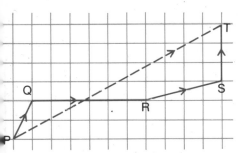

C1 (a) Write down the column vectors for $\vec{PQ}$, $\vec{QR}$, $\vec{RS}$ and $\vec{ST}$.

(b) Add the four column vectors together.

(c) Check that the result is the column vector for $\vec{PT}$.

C2 In this diagram, $\vec{AB} = \begin{bmatrix} 4 \\ -2 \end{bmatrix}$ and $\vec{BC} = \begin{bmatrix} -1 \\ -3 \end{bmatrix}$.

Work out $\begin{bmatrix} 4 \\ -2 \end{bmatrix} + \begin{bmatrix} -1 \\ -3 \end{bmatrix}$ and check that the

result is the column vector of $\vec{AC}$.

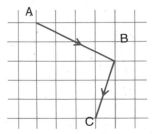

C3 Calculate each of these and draw vector diagrams to illustrate. The first is done as an example.

(a) $\begin{bmatrix} 5 \\ -2 \end{bmatrix} + \begin{bmatrix} -3 \\ -4 \end{bmatrix} = \begin{bmatrix} 2 \\ -6 \end{bmatrix}$

(b) $\begin{bmatrix} -3 \\ -4 \end{bmatrix} + \begin{bmatrix} -2 \\ 6 \end{bmatrix}$

(c) $\begin{bmatrix} 3 \\ -7 \end{bmatrix} + \begin{bmatrix} -5 \\ 2 \end{bmatrix}$

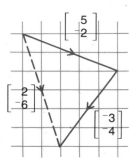

29

C4 Work these out.

(a) $\begin{bmatrix} 3 \\ 2 \end{bmatrix} + \begin{bmatrix} ^-1 \\ 4 \end{bmatrix}$ (b) $\begin{bmatrix} ^-3 \\ 5 \end{bmatrix} + \begin{bmatrix} 2 \\ ^-1 \end{bmatrix}$ (c) $\begin{bmatrix} ^-4 \\ ^-5 \end{bmatrix} + \begin{bmatrix} 0 \\ ^-2 \end{bmatrix}$

(d) $\begin{bmatrix} ^-2 \\ ^-2 \end{bmatrix} + \begin{bmatrix} ^-3 \\ ^-1 \end{bmatrix}$ (e) $\begin{bmatrix} 0 \\ ^-6 \end{bmatrix} + \begin{bmatrix} 4 \\ 6 \end{bmatrix}$ (f) $\begin{bmatrix} 3 \\ ^-8 \end{bmatrix} + \begin{bmatrix} ^-7 \\ ^-1 \end{bmatrix}$

C5 This diagram was drawn on squared paper, but most of the squares have been rubbed out.

Without using squared paper yourself, work out the column vector for

(a) $\overrightarrow{AC}$ (b) $\overrightarrow{DC}$

(c) $\overrightarrow{EC}$ (d) $\overrightarrow{BE}$

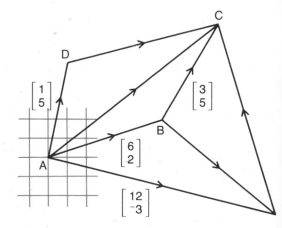

D Translations

The girl in this picture is about to move the table.

She drags it across the floor without rotating it. We say the table has been **translated**.

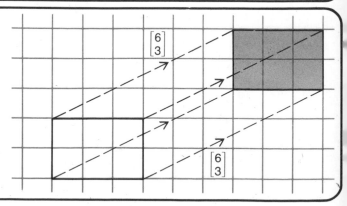

We can use a column vector to describe a translation.

In this diagram every point of the table moves along a vector $\begin{bmatrix} 6 \\ 3 \end{bmatrix}$.

$\begin{bmatrix} 6 \\ 3 \end{bmatrix}$ is the column vector of the translation.

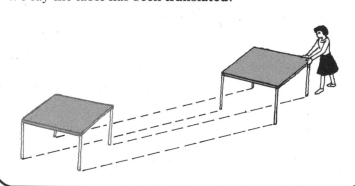

D1 The left-hand set of points is translated onto the right-hand set.

What is the column vector of the translation?

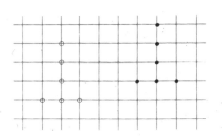

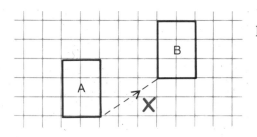

D2 Sam said that the column vector of the translation from shape A to shape B is $\begin{bmatrix} 3 \\ 2 \end{bmatrix}$.

He is wrong. What is the column vector of the translation?

D3 Copy this diagram on squared paper. Translate the shape using the column vector $\begin{bmatrix} 4 \\ -1 \end{bmatrix}$.

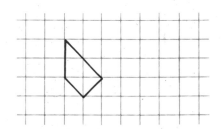

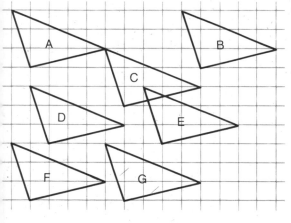

D4 Write down the column vector of each of these translations.

(a) A to B   (b) A to C

(c) A to F   (d) E to A

(e) B to E   (f) G to E

(g) C to E   (h) E to C

(i) D to E   (j) B to A

D5 (a) Write down the column vector of the translation F to D in the diagram above.

(b) Write down the column vector of the translation D to C.

(c) Add the two column vectors together. The result should be the column vector of the translation F to C.

E Translation symmetry

Dress materials and wallpapers often have a **repeating pattern** on them.

A repeating pattern is based on a grid of parallelograms.

You have to think of the pattern as extending outwards in all directions, without end. We call such a pattern an **infinite** pattern.

If you make a tracing of a repeating pattern, . . .

. . . you can translate the tracing so that it fits over the pattern again. (Remember the pattern is infinite).

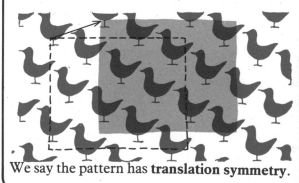

We say the pattern has **translation symmetry**.

E1 Imagine that you have a tracing of this infinite pattern.

(a) You translate the tracing so that flower A fits over flower F. Which flower does flower E fit over?

(b) What is the column vector of the translation in part (a)?

(c) Write down the column vectors of **three** other translations, each of which will move the tracing so that it fits over the pattern.

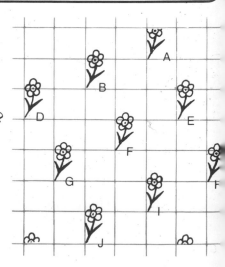

The pattern shown here has

(1) **reflection symmetry**

Every dashed line is a line of reflection symmetry.

(2) **rotation symmetry**

Every point marked with a dot is a 2-fold rotation centre. If the pattern is rotated through 180° about any of these points, it will fit onto itself.

(3) **translation symmetry**

The arrow shows one translation which moves the pattern onto itself.

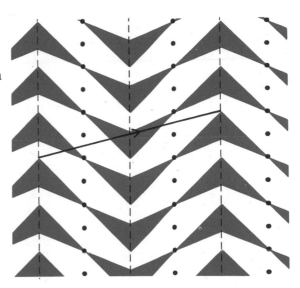

E2 *You need worksheet Y3–1.*

For each pattern, find two different translations which move the pattern onto itself, and draw their vectors. Also mark any lines of reflection symmetry or centres of rotation symmetry.

(a)

(b)

(c)

(d)

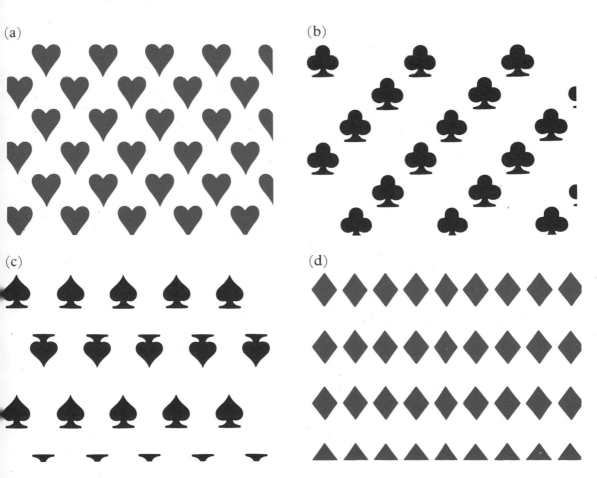

Algebra review (1)

1 These arrangements are made with red and black balls joined together.

(a) How many black balls will there be in an arrangement of this kind with 20 red balls?

(b) If there are *r* red balls and *b* black balls in one of these arrangements, write a formula for *b* in terms of *r*.

(c) Re-arrange the formula to give *r* in terms of *b*. Check that your new formula gives the correct result for each of the arrangements shown above.

2 A container whose mass is *c* grams contains *v* millilitres of a liquid. The mass of 1 millilitre of the liquid is *r* grams. Write an expression for the total mass of the container and the liquid.

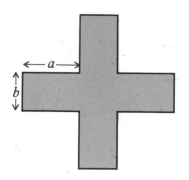

3 The four 'arms' of this cross are of equal length *a* and equal width *b*.

Write down an expression for

(a) the perimeter of the shape

(b) the area of the shape

4 Simplify these expressions, where possible.

(a) $3a - 2 + 5a - 3$ (b) $10 - 2x - 4 + 7x$ (c) $2s - 5 - 6s + 7$

(d) $2a^2 - 3a + 4 + a$ (e) $p + pq - 3 - p^2$ (f) $5 - 3y - 8 - y$

5 Remove the brackets from these expressions, and simplify.

(a) $4x - (3 + x)$ (b) $5 + (3a - 1)$ (c) $2y - (y - 3)$

(d) $20 - (4s + 5)$ (e) $8t - (6 - 2t)$ (f) $3u - (7u - 2)$

6 Write down an expression, without brackets, for the length of the red part of this strip.

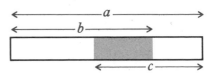

7 Solve each of these equations.

(a) $13x - 23 = 68$ (b) $70 - 8x = 14$ (c) $5x = 45 - 4x$

(d) $\dfrac{x}{3} + 12 = 29$ (e) $7 = \dfrac{x}{5} - 8$ (f) $16 - \dfrac{x}{6} = 2$

8 Multiply out the brackets in each of these expressions.

(a) $(x + 5)(y + 3)$ (b) $(x + 5)(x + 3)$ (c) $(x - 7)(x - 2)$

(d) $(x - 4)(x - 9)$ (e) $(2x - 3)(x + 1)$ (f) $(5x + 4)(2x - 3)$

9 (a) Write down six consecutive whole numbers, for example

$$4 \quad 5 \quad 6 \quad 7 \quad 8 \quad 9$$

Find the product of the first and sixth numbers: $4 \times 9 = 36$.
Find the product of the second and fifth numbers: $5 \times 8 = 40$.

Do this for other sets of six consecutive whole numbers.
What do you notice about the results?

(b) Let n be the first of six consecutive whole numbers. The second number will be $n + 1$.

(i) Write down expressions for the third, fourth, fifth and sixth numbers.

(ii) Write down an expression for the product of the first and sixth numbers, and for the product of the second and fifth numbers.

(iii) Multiply out your expressions in (ii) and thus explain the result you found in part (a).

10 Make the letter printed in red the subject of each formula.

(a) $y = a + bx$ (b) $t = \dfrac{s + m}{a}$ (c) $t = \dfrac{s + m}{a}$

(d) $w = \dfrac{u - v}{c}$ (e) $w = \dfrac{u - v}{c}$ (f) $r = \dfrac{x}{a} - e$

11 The formula for changing temperatures in degrees Celsius to degrees Fahrenheit is $f = 1{\cdot}8c + 32$, where f is the Fahrenheit temperature and c the Celsius temperature.

A rough rule for converting Celsius to Fahrenheit is $f = 2c + 30$.

For what temperature in degrees Celsius does the rough rule give the correct Fahrenheit temperature?

4 Percentage (1)

A Comparison

Percentages are often used to make a comparison fairer.

A gardener bought two packets of onion seeds, A and B.
Packet A contained 46 seeds; packet B contained 37 seeds.
She planted both lots of seeds. 32 of the A-seeds germinated
(grew into plants) and 28 of the B-seeds.

It would not be fair to say that because 32 is greater than 28, then
packet A is better than packet B. There were more A-seeds to start
with, so we would expect more A-seeds than B-seeds to germinate,
even if both packets were equally good.

So which is better, 32 out of 46,

or 28 out of 37?

We use percentages to settle this question.

$\frac{32}{46} = 0{\cdot}70$ (to 2 d.p.) = **70%** $\frac{28}{37} = 0{\cdot}76$ (to 2 d.p.) = **76%**

So 28 out of 37 is better.

When we use percentages in this
way, we are comparing A and B
by comparing both with a scale
going from 0 to 100.

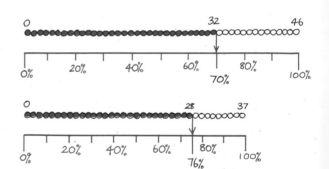

Although 28 out of 37 is better than 32 out of 46, it does not follow that
the B-seeds were better seeds than the A-seeds. They performed better, but
there may be all kinds of reasons for that. Perhaps they were planted in
richer soil, or perhaps they had more rain.

By using **percentages** to compare how the seeds performed we have
allowed for the fact that **different numbers of seeds were planted**.
But that is all we have allowed for. We have not allowed for any
differences in soil, climate, and so on.

36

You will need a pie chart scale for some of these questions.

A1 At the 1981 census, the total population of the UK (to the nearest thousand) was 55 039 000, of whom 28 261 000 were female. In the Republic of Ireland there were 1 729 000 males and 1 714 000 females.

Calculate the percentage of females in each of the two countries.

A2 This table shows how the land area of the UK and Ireland is split up into various kinds of use.

Land use	Number of square miles in UK	Number of square miles in Ireland
Arable and permanent crops (including orchards)	27 000	4 000
Permanent pasture	44 900	14 700
Forest and wood	7 800	800
Other uses	13 600	7 000
Total land area	93 300	26 500

(a) For each country, calculate the percentage of the total land area taken up by each land use.

(b) Draw two pie charts to show how the land is divided up between uses in the two countries.

A3 These tables show the numbers of votes given to each party in the general elections in 1979 and 1983 (excluding Northern Ireland). The numbers are rounded off to the nearest 10 000.

1979

Conservative	13 700 000
Labour	11 510 000
Liberal	4 310 000
Others	1 020 000

1983

Conservative	13 010 000
Labour	8 460 000
Liberal/SDP	7 780 000
Others	660 000

(a) For each election, calculate the percentage of the total votes given to each party.

(b) Draw two pie charts, one for each election.

(c) If there has been another general election since 1983, find out the figures for that election and draw a pie chart.

B Two-way tables

Subdividing means splitting into groups. For example, the population
of a town or country can be subdivided into groups according to age.
It could be subdivided into several groups (for example, 0–9, 10–19, and
so on) or into just two groups (for example, 'under 65' and '65 or over').

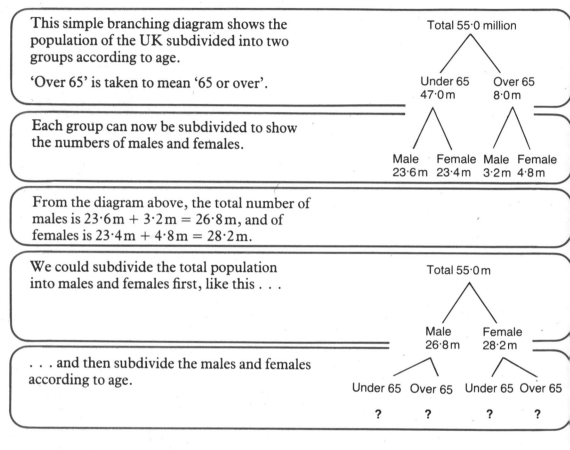

This simple branching diagram shows the
population of the UK subdivided into two
groups according to age.

'Over 65' is taken to mean '65 or over'.

Total 55·0 million

Under 65   Over 65
47·0 m   8·0 m

Each group can now be subdivided to show
the numbers of males and females.

Male   Female   Male   Female
23·6 m 23·4 m   3·2 m 4·8 m

From the diagram above, the total number of
males is 23·6 m + 3·2 m = 26·8 m, and of
females is 23·4 m + 4·8 m = 28·2 m.

We could subdivide the total population
into males and females first, like this . . .

Total 55·0 m

Male   Female
26·8 m   28·2 m

. . . and then subdivide the males and females
according to age.

Under 65   Over 65   Under 65   Over 65

?   ?   ?   ?

B1 What numbers go along the bottom of the second branching
diagram?

The population of the UK has been subdivided in the diagrams above
by **age** and by **sex**. This is called a **two-way** subdivision. It results
in four subgroups:

    Males under 65   Males over 65   Females under 65   Females over 65

Another way to show the two-way subdivision
is by a **two-way table**.

The rows are labelled to show one way of
subdividing the population.
The columns are labelled to show the other
way of subdividing the population.

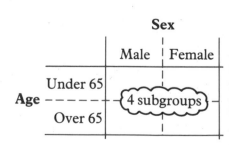

38

This two-way table shows the number in each of the four subgroups.

It also shows the total of each row, the total of each column, and the 'grand total' (55·0 million).

Age	Sex Male	Sex Female	Total
Under 65	23·6m	23·4m	47·0m
Over 65	3·2m	4·8m	8·0m
Total	26·8m	28·2m	55·0m

There are various comparisons we can make by calculating percentages from the numbers in the two-way table. We may want to know

1 what percentage of the total population fall into each of the four subgroups;

2 what percentage of each age-group are males, and what percentage are females;

3 what percentage of each sex are under 65 and what percentage are over 65.

When you calculate a percentage, it is important to say what it is a percentage of.

1 What percentage of the population are in each subgroup?

Start with the subgroup of males under 65.
There are 23·6m in a total population of 55·0m.

$$\frac{23·6}{55·0} = 0·429 \quad \text{(to 3 d.p.)}$$

So males under 65 are **42·9%** of the population.

We can show this in a new table.

	Male	Female	Total
Under 65	42·9%		
Over 65			
Total			100% (55·0m)

This '100%' refers to the total population. The actual figure is written in brackets after it.

It is a good idea to write the actual total in this way. It enables someone to calculate all the other actual figures if they want them.

B2 Copy the table. Calculate the percentage of the total population in each of the other three subgroups, to the nearest 0·1%, and fill them in. Fill in the row totals and the column totals.

When you add up to get the 'grand total' of all four subgroups, you will find it comes to 99·9%. This is because each percentage was rounded off. You still write '100%' in the table.

B3 Do the same as in question B2 for this table. It shows a breakdown of the population of Italy.

	Male	Female	Total
Under 65	24·7m	24·7m	49·4m
Over 65	3·2m	4·5m	7·7m
Total	27·9m	29·2m	57·1m

B4 Look at the percentage tables for the UK and Italy. Comment on any similarities or big differences.

2 What percentage of each age-group are male, and what percentage are female?

Here again is the two-way table for the UK, showing the actual figures.

Take the 'under 65' age-group first. There are 47·0m in this age-group. Of these, 23·6m are male.

	Male	Female	Total
Under 65	23·6m	23·4m	47·0m
Over 65	3·2m	4·8m	8·0m
Total	26·8m	28·2m	55·0m

$$\frac{23\cdot6}{47\cdot0} = 0\cdot502 \text{ (to 3 d.p.)} = 50\cdot2\%$$

So **50·2%** of the under 65s are male. It follows that **49·8%** are female.

We can do similar calculations for the 'over 65' age-group. The percentages are shown in this table.

	Male	Female	Total
Under 65	50·2%	49·8%	100% (47·0m)
Over 65	40·0%	60·0%	100% (8·0m)

Notice that there is **no total of each column**. It would not make sense to add, for example, the 50·2% and the 40·0% in the first column. They are **percentages of two different amounts**. The 50·2% is a percentage of the 'under 65' group, while the 40·0% is a percentage of the 'over 65' group.

We make clear what each percentage is a percentage of, by writing '100%' in the table where it is a total. The actual figure is written in brackets after it.

The percentage table can be used to compare the two age-groups. The percentages of males in the two age-groups are very different. Males make up just over a half of the under 65 group, but less than 40% of the 'over 65' group.

B5 Look back at the table for Italy in question B3.
Make a table showing the percentages of males and of females
in each age group.

Is the table similar to that of the UK, or very different?

3 What percentage of each sex are under 65, and what percentage are over 65?

Here once again is the two-way table for
the UK, with the actual figures in
each subgroup.

	Male	Female	Total
Under 65	23·6m	23·4m	47·0m
Over 65	3·2m	4·8m	8·0m
Total	26·8m	28·2m	55·0m

Take the males first. There are 26·8m.
Of these 23·6m are under 65.

$$\frac{23·6}{26·8} = 0·881 \text{ (to 3 d.p.)} = 88·1\%$$

So **88·1%** of the males are under 65. It follows that **11·9%** are over 65.

Similar calculations can be done for the females.
The percentages are shown in this table.

	Male	Female
Under 65	88·1%	83·0%
Over 65	11·9%	17·0%
Total	100%	100%
	(26·8m)	(28·2m)

This time there is **no total of each row**, for the same sort of reason
as before.

This table allows us to compare the sexes. A larger percentage of the
females than of the males are over 65.

B6 Make a similar table for the population of Italy,
using the figures given in question B3.

B7 Use the tables you have made in this section to answer
these questions about the UK and Italy.

(a) Which country has the higher percentage of over 65s
amongst its females?

(b) Which country has the higher percentage of females
amongst its over 65s?

(c) Which country has the higher percentage of males
amongst its under 65s?

(d) Which country has the higher percentage of under 65s
amonst its males?

41

c Interpreting accident statistics

C1 This data is taken from a report on road accidents produced by Essex Police. The table shows the number of accidents resulting in injury or death in each quarter of one year.

	Slight injury	Serious injury	Fatal
1st quarter (Jan., Feb., Mar.)	979	441	26
2nd quarter (Apr., May, June)	1042	489	39
3rd quarter (July, Aug., Sept.)	1139	483	33
4th quarter (Oct., Nov., Dec.)	1184	552	43

(a) Make a table showing what percentage of the accidents in each quarter involved slight injury, what percentage involved serious injury and what percentage were fatal.

(b) Make another table showing what percentage of each kind of accident happened in the 1st quarter, the 2nd quarter, and so on.

(c) Do the figures show that it is safer to drive in the 1st quarter than in the 2nd, 3rd or 4th?

C2 The Essex Police report also gives the number of accidents which took place at various different kinds of location.

Location	No. of accidents	Location	No. of accidents
Ordinary road (at least 20 m from a junction)	2806	Roundabout	314
		'Y' junction	134
'T' or staggered junction	2057	Slip road	52
Crossroads	499	Multiple junction	40
Private drive/entrance	478	Other junction	70

(a) Calculate the percentage of accidents which happened on ordinary road.

(b) Do the same for accidents which happened at crossroads.

(c) The percentage of accidents which happened on ordinary road is higher than the percentage for any of the other locations. Does it follow that an ordinary road is a more dangerous place than a junction or crossroads, etc.?

Accident statistics are often misunderstood. The data in question C1 does not show that it is safer to drive in the 1st quarter. Although there are fewer accidents in the 1st quarter, there are generally fewer drivers around as well. For all we know, it may be that nearly all the drivers who drove in the 1st quarter had accidents!

The data in question C2 does not show that an ordinary road is the most dangerous kind of place to drive on. The data was collected for the whole of Essex, and the amount of ordinary road is much greater than the amount of crossroads, etc. So even if every spot were **equally** dangerous, we would still expect more accidents to occur on ordinary road.

C3 The report also contains this information about the number
of accidents which occurred on each of the principal roads
in Essex, together with the length of that road in the county.

Road	No. of accidents	Length in km
A12	181	68
A13	310	57
A120	113	46
A127	134	30
A128	130	33
A130	190	52
A131	65	35
A133	103	29
A414	130	51
A604	110	73
M11	42	32

It would not be fair to compare the roads using the number of
accidents alone, because the roads are of different lengths. It would
not be fair to compare the number of accidents on a road 100 km
long with the number on a road only 10 km long.

(a) Can you think of a way to make the comparison between roads fairer?
Use your method to put the roads into an order, with the
road with the worst accident record first.

(b) You have allowed for the different lengths in making the comparison.
What other reasons could there be why one road is worse than another?

C4 The wearing of seat belts was not compulsory in 1980.
This table shows a breakdown of the number of accidents to
drivers and front seat passengers in Essex in 1980.

	Serious/fatal injury	Slight injury	Total
Wearing belt	178	686	864
Not wearing belt	636	1502	2138

What conclusions would you draw from this data?
Explain how you arrive at your conclusion. If you do any
calculations to help you decide your answer, show what
calculations you do.

C5 A motoring magazine published figures that 75% of
drivers involved in accidents had not been drinking, and only
25% had been drinking. Some people drew the conclusion that
it was much safer to drink and drive than not to drink and
drive. Were they right to draw this conclusion from the data?
If not, why not?

5 Mappings

A Reflection

The triangle ABC has been reflected in the dotted line, to give the triangle A′ B′ C′.

The triangle ABC in its starting position is called the **object** of the reflection. The result of reflecting the object is called the **image**.

We also use the words **object** and **image** when talking about individual points.
For example, A is an object and A′ its image.

(When a letter is used to name a point, then the image is usually shown by using the same letter with a dash.)

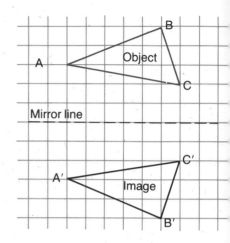

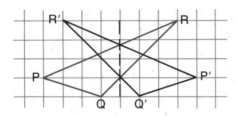

In mathematics we always think of mirrors as being double-sided.

Points on one side are reflected on to the other, and vice versa.

It is easy to reflect a point in a mirror which is on a grid line, by counting squares.

When the mirror line is at 45° to the grid lines, we can count squares diagonally.

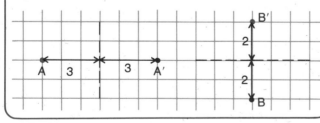

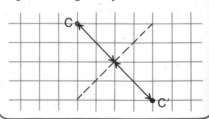

A1 Copy each diagram and reflect the shape in the dotted line.

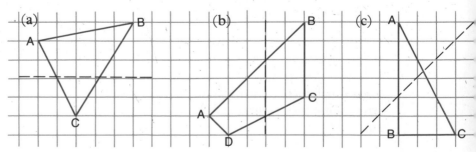

44

A2 This diagram shows the line whose equation is $y = x$. Copy the diagram.

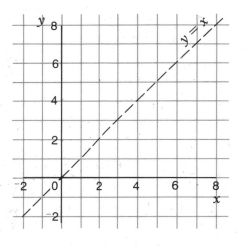

(a) Copy the table below. Mark the five object points on your diagram and find their images. Write the images in the table.

Object	Image
(7, 3)	
(2, 4)	
(0, 4)	
(⁻2, 1)	
(⁻1, 6)	

(b) What is the relationship between the coordinates of an object and the coordinates of its image?

(c) Use this relationship to write down the image of each of these points after reflection in $y = x$.

(i) (13, 19)   (ii) (⁻6, 18)   (iii) (⁻4, ⁻10)   (iv) (a, b)

A3 This diagram shows the line whose equation is $x = 5$.

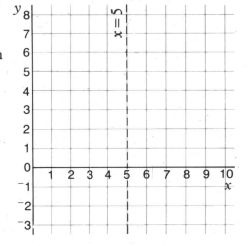

(a) Copy and complete this table, which shows some points and their images after reflection in $x = 5$.

Object	Image
(4, 3)	
(2, 5)	
(1, ⁻2)	
(7, 6)	
(5, 1)	

(b) The y-coordinate of each image is the same as the y-coordinate of the object.
There is a relationship between the x-coordinate of each object and the x-coordinate of its image. What is this relationship?

(c) Use the relationship to work out the image of each of these points.

(i) (3, 20)   (ii) (6, ⁻8)   (iii) (0, 7)   (iv) (⁻1, 5)   (v) (13, 4)

A4 Let (a, b) be the coordinates of an object point.
Write down, in terms of a and b, the coordinates of the image of (a, b) after reflection in $x = 5$ (as in question A3).

B 180° rotation

You need worksheet Y3–2, tracing paper.

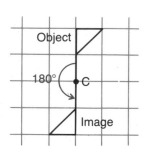

In this diagram the upright flag has been rotated
through 180° about the point C.

The flag in its starting position is called the **object**
of the rotation. The new position is called the **image**.

The point C is called the **centre of rotation**.

The centre of rotation does not have to be a point
on the object itself.

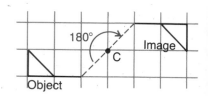

The example below shows how tracing paper can be used to find the
position of an image after a 180° rotation.

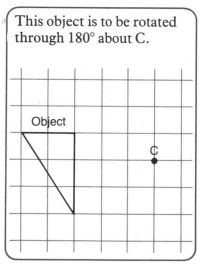

This object is to be rotated
through 180° about C.

Trace the object and the centre of rotation.
Then rotate the tracing through 180° (half
a complete turn) keeping the point C fixed.

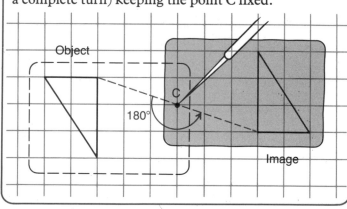

The diagrams for questions B1 to B4 are on worksheet Y3–2.

B1 In each case draw the image of the object after a 180° rotation
about C. Use tracing paper if you wish.

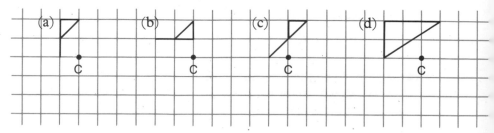

B2 Each diagram below shows an object together with its image after a 180° rotation. Mark the centre of rotation in each case.

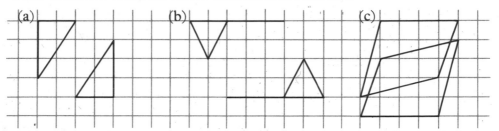

(a) (b) (c)

B3 Draw the image of each object after a 180° rotation about C.
Do it without using tracing paper.

(a) (b) (c)

(d) (e) (f)

Here is a simple way to find the image of a point after a 180° rotation.

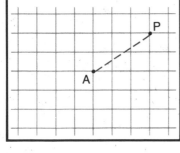

| P is to be rotated through 180° about A as centre. | Draw, or think of, an L-shape between A and P. | Rotate the L-shape to find where P goes. |

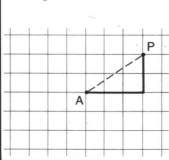

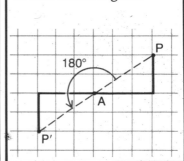

B4 Use the L-shape method to find the image of each point P, Q and R after a 180° rotation about A.
Then join up P', Q', R' to make the image of triangle PQR.

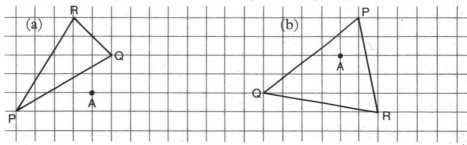

(a) (b)

C 90° rotation

You need worksheet Y3–3, tracing paper.

This diagram shows how tracing paper
can be used to find the image of an object
after a 90° rotation about a centre.

In this case the rotation is **anticlockwise**.

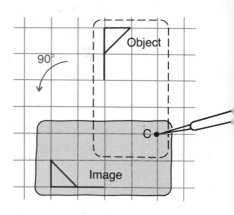

The diagrams for questions C1 to C5 are on worksheet Y3–3.

C1 In each case draw the image of the object after a rotation
of 90° anticlockwise about C. Use tracing paper if you wish.

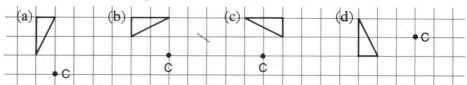

C2 *Without using tracing paper*, draw the image of each object
after a rotation of 90° anticlockwise about C. Afterwards
check your answers with tracing paper.

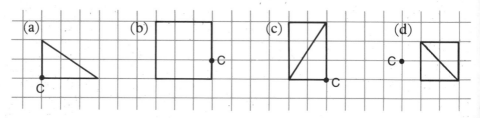

The L-shape method can also be used for a 90° rotation.

P is to be rotated through 90° anticlockwise about A.	Think of, or draw, the L-shape, as before.	Rotate the L-shape to find where P goes to.

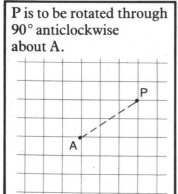 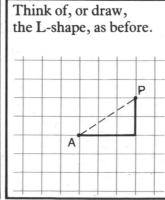 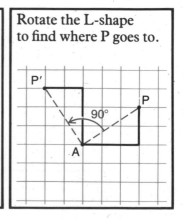

48

C3 (a) Find the image of P after a 90° anticlockwise rotation about A. Label it P′.

(b) Rotate P′ through 90° anticlockwise about A, and mark the image P″.

(c) Rotate P″ in the same way to get P‴.

(d) Join up PP′P″P‴. What shape is it and where is A in relation to it?

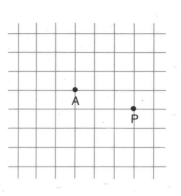

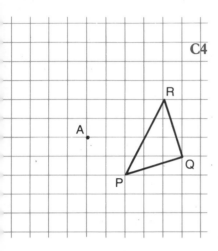

C4 (a) Use the L-shape method to rotate each point P, Q, R though 90° anticlockwise about A. Join up P′Q′R′.

(b) Rotate P′Q′R′ in the same way to get P″Q″R″.

(c) Rotate P″Q″R″ in the same way to get P‴Q‴R‴.

(d) What kind of symmetry does the pattern of four triangles have?

C5 Each diagram shows an object and its image after a 90° rotation. The rotation may be clockwise or anticlockwise. In each case the image is shaded.

See if you can find the centre of each rotation. Use tracing paper to check when you think you may have found the centre.

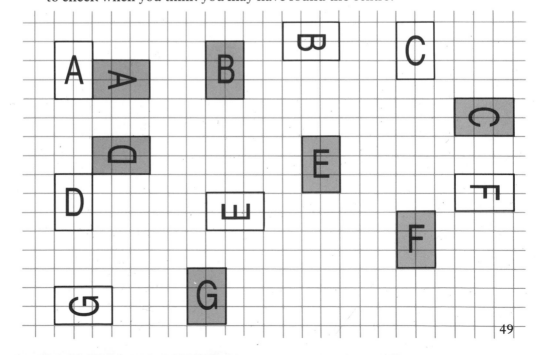

D Translation

In a translation, every point moves the same distance and in the same direction.

A translation can be described by a column vector. The diagram on the right shows a translation whose vector is $\begin{bmatrix} 4 \\ -2 \end{bmatrix}$.

Once again the new position of a point is called its image.

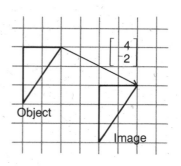

D1 What is the column vector of each of these translations? The **image** is shaded in each case.

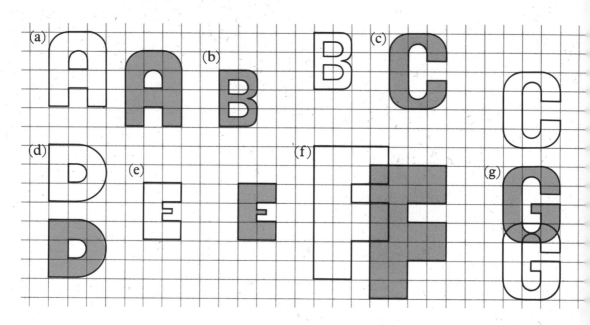

(a) (b) (c) (d) (e) (f) (g)

E Congruence

Congruent means 'having the same shape and the same size'.

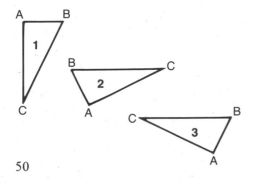

E1 Triangles 1, 2 and 3 are congruent. Trace triangle 1.

(a) Can you fit your tracing over triangle 2 without turning the tracing paper over? What about triangle 3?

(b) The lettering of triangle 1 goes clockwise round the triangle. Which way does it go on triangle 2? Which way on triangle 3?

50

We say that triangle 1 (at the bottom of the previous page) is
directly congruent to triangle 2, but **oppositely congruent** to triangle 3.

E2 This question is easy to do if you use tracing paper.
Do it without tracing paper.

For each shape below say whether it is
directly congruent or oppositely congruent
to the shape shown on the right.

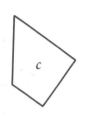

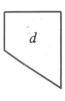

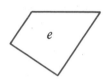

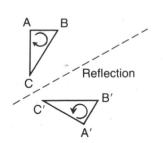

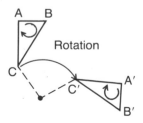

F Mappings

A reflection can be thought of as a 'machine'.
The inputs are objects and the outputs are images.

When a reflection is thought of in this way, it
is called a **mapping**, and we say each object
is **mapped onto** its image.

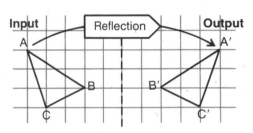

A reflection produces an image which is oppositely congruent to the
object. The **sense** of the lettering is changed (from clockwise to anticlockwise, or vice versa).

Rotations and translations are also mappings. They produce an image
which is directly congruent to the object.

In the diagrams below, ⟲ and ⟳ show the sense of the lettering.

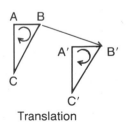

51

In some questions below you are asked to describe a mapping.
You first say whether it is a reflection, a rotation or a translation.
If it is a reflection, you give the mirror line (e.g. its equation).
If it is a rotation, you give the centre, angle and sense (clockwise or anticlockwise).
If it is a translation, you give the column vector.

F1 (a) Which triangles are directly congruent to triangle 1?

(b) Which triangles are oppositely congruent to triangle 1?

(c) Describe the mapping which maps triangle 1 onto

    (i) triangle 3

    (ii) triangle 5

    (iii) triangle 6

    (iv) triangle 8

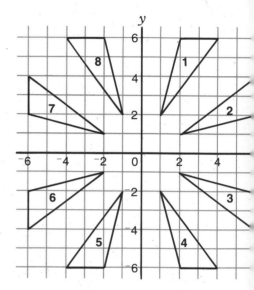

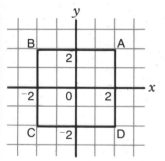

F2 The square ABCD shown on the left is the object.
Each diagram below shows the image of ABCD after a mapping.
Describe the mapping in each case.

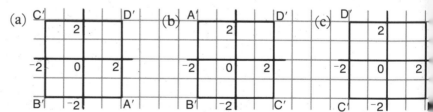

The diagrams for questions F3 to F9 are on worksheet Y3–4.

F3 ABCD is the square cross-section of a heavy box standing on the floor.
The box is rolled along the floor. First it is rotated about A as shown, until B is on the floor. Then it is rotated about the new position of B, and so on until it is the same way up as before.

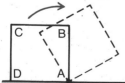

Draw and letter each position of the box, and draw the path traced out by the point D as the box rolls.

52

F4 This is a **plan** showing a heavy cupboard PQRS standing against a wall. The cupboard is moved as follows:

(1) It is first rotated 90° anticlockwise about R;
(2) then it is rotated 90° clockwise about the new position of S;
(3) then it is rotated 90° clockwise about the new position of R;
(4) finally it is rotated 90° anticlockwise about the new position of S.

Draw and letter each intermediate position of the cupboard, and the final position.

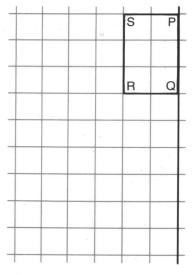

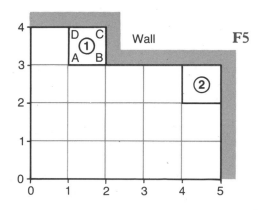

F5 A safe, labelled ABCD in this plan, is to be moved from position 1 to position 2. It is very heavy and it is only possible to move it by rotating about any one corner.

Show how the safe can be moved from position 1 to position 2. Draw and label each intermediate position. Label the final position.

Describe each mapping.

F6

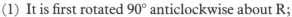

(a) Reflect triangle ABC in line 1. Label the image A′B′C′.

(b) Reflect triangle A′B′C′ in line 2. Label the image A″B″C″.

(c) Describe the single mapping which maps ABC onto A″B″C″.

F7 Use a new copy of the diagram given in question F6.

(a) Reflect triangle ABC first in line 2. Label the image A′B′C′.

(b) Reflect A′B′C′ in line 1. Label the image A″B″C″.

(c) Describe the single mapping which maps ABC onto A″B″C″.

When you stand between two parallel mirrors which face each other you can see a sequence of images, alternately facing you and facing away from you.

We shall now see why this happens.

There are in fact two sequences of images.
To get the first sequence we start by reflecting the person in mirror 1, to get image 1.
Image 1 is then reflected in mirror 2 to get image 1,2.
Image 1,2 is reflected in mirror 1 to get image 1,2,1; and so on.

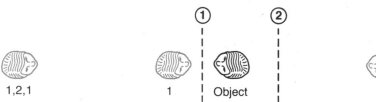

For the second sequence we start by reflecting the person in mirror 2, to get image 2.
Image 2 is reflected in mirror 1 to get image 2,1.
Image 2,1 is reflected in mirror 2 to get image 2,1,2; and so on.

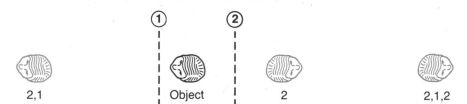

When the two sequences are put together, we get this.

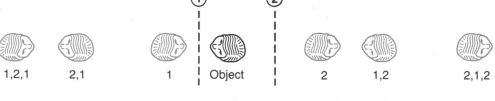

If the mirrors are moved so that they are no longer parallel, this is the effect on the images.

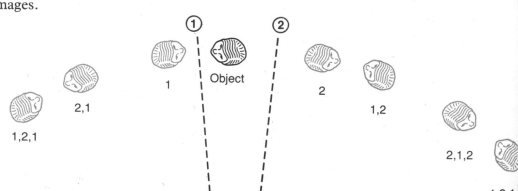

By adjusting the angle between the mirrors, we can make the images form a closed 'ring'.

In this example the angle between the mirrors is 30°.

A 'kaleidoscope' works in this way. The angle between the mirrors is usually 60°.

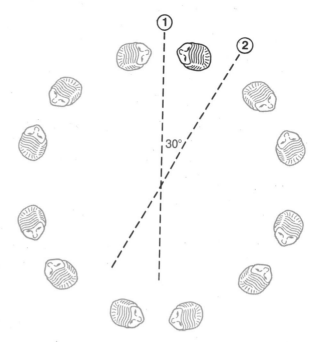

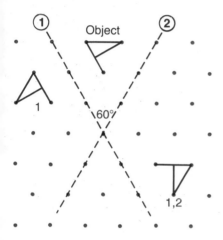

F8 In this diagram, the angle between the mirrors is 60°.

Images 1 and 1,2 are already drawn.

Complete the diagram by drawing and labelling these images:

1,2,1   2   2,1

*F9 (a) Draw and label the complete set of images for this diagram.

The angle between the mirrors is 72°.

(b) Now get two mirrors and place them in position along the lines so that they meet at the centre of the circle.

How many images do you see?

Why can you not see all of the images you have drawn?

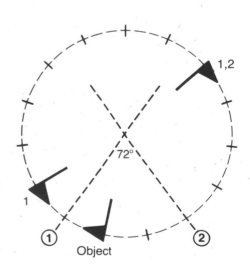

55

6 Investigations (1)

1   This is a drawing of three bricks in a row.
You should be able to find 6 rectangles in
the drawing.

Investigate the number of rectangles when there are four, five, etc.
bricks in a row.

Try to explain why the number of rectangles increases as it does.

2   Take a strip of paper.

Fold it in half, left over right.

Fold again, left over right.

Fold again, left over right.

Open out, and you will see a pattern of folds.
Those marked D point down ∨ and those marked U point up ∧.

U   U   D   D   U   D   D

Investigate the way in which the pattern of folds builds up
as you fold the strip in half each time.

See if you can work out what the pattern will be after the strip
has been folded in half 5 times, without actually folding.

3   Investigate how the pattern of folds builds up when a square piece
of paper is folded in half, in half again, and again, like this.

See if you can work out what the pattern will be after the square
has been folded in half 5 times, without actually folding.

Review 1

1 Stretching and enlargement

1.1 This rectangle is to be stretched across to make a square.
What stretch factor will be needed?

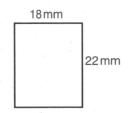

1.2 The ellipse shown in this diagram is made by stretching the dotted circle.

(a) Calculate the stretch factor.

(b) Calculate the area of the ellipse.

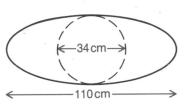

1.3 A photo whose area is $54\,\text{cm}^2$ is enlarged using a scale factor of 3.
Calculate the area of the enlargement.

1.4 A picture whose area is $18 \cdot 5\,\text{cm}^2$ is reduced using a scale factor of $0 \cdot 8$.
Calculate the area of the reduced picture.

1.5 In an office there is a photocopier which is capable of reducing diagrams using scale factors $0 \cdot 9, 0 \cdot 8, 0 \cdot 7, 0 \cdot 6, 0 \cdot 5, 0 \cdot 4$ or $0 \cdot 3$.

(a) Which of these scale factors would you use if you wanted the area of the reduced diagram to be as near as possible to $\frac{1}{2}$ of that of the original? Explain why.

(b) Which would you use to get the area of the reduction to be as near as possible to $\frac{1}{3}$ of that of the original? Explain why.

2 Linear relationships

2.1 Write down the gradient of each of the lines in this diagram.

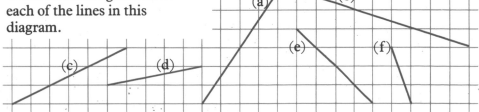

2.2 Find the gradient of the line through
(a) $(0, 0)$ and $(3, 2)$
(b) $(1, 6)$ and $(5, 4)$
(c) $(^-1, 3)$ and $(2, 6)$
(d) $(3, {}^-2)$ and $(8, 4)$
(e) $(^-2, 7)$ and $(3, {}^-3)$
(f) $(^-1, {}^-1)$ and $(4, 8)$

2.3 Write down the equation of each line shown here.

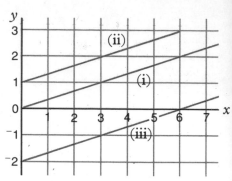

2.4 Write down   (i) the gradient,   (ii) the intercept on the y-axis, of each of these graphs.

(a) $y = 3x - 5$ (b) $y = 6 + 2x$ (c) $y = 10 - 4x$ (d) $2x + y = 12$

2.5 (a) What is the gradient of line (i) in this diagram?

(b) Write down the equation of each line.

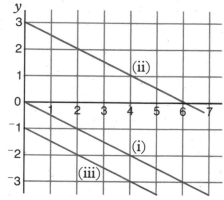

2.6 (a) Choose two points on this graph and use them to find the gradient of the line (as a decimal).

(b) Write down the equation of the line in gradient–intercept form. $(y = \ldots x + \ldots)$

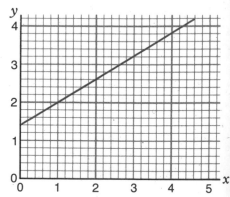

2.7 A student connected a battery to various pieces of apparatus. In each case she measured the current, I amps, and the voltage, V volts, across the terminals of the apparatus. These were her results.

I	3·0	5·5	7·5	8·6	10·0
V	7·8	6·9	5·9	5·5	5·1

(a) Draw axes with I across and V up. Plot the four points. Draw a line of best fit through them.

(b) Find the equation of your line.

3 Vectors

3.1 A plane flies from A to B to C.

$\overrightarrow{AB}$ is 50 km on a bearing 345°. $\overrightarrow{BC}$ is 50 km on a bearing 105°.

Find the length and bearing of $\overrightarrow{AC}$.

3.2 Work out   (a) $\begin{bmatrix} ^-6 \\ 1 \end{bmatrix} + \begin{bmatrix} 4 \\ ^-3 \end{bmatrix}$ (b) $\begin{bmatrix} 7 \\ 2 \end{bmatrix} + \begin{bmatrix} ^-2 \\ ^-7 \end{bmatrix}$ (c) $\begin{bmatrix} ^-3 \\ ^-8 \end{bmatrix} + \begin{bmatrix} ^-2 \\ 4 \end{bmatrix}$

3.3 This map shows a boat trip round an island.
The journey starts and finishes at A.

(a) Write down each column vector in the journey.

(b) Add all the column vectors together.

(c) Can you explain why you get your answer?

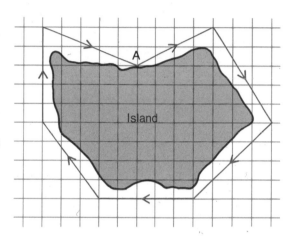

4 Percentage (1)

4.1 The table below is taken from an old mathematics book.
It claims to show the number of people in the armed services
of various countries in 1915, together with the population of
each country at that time.

Country	Population	Number in armed services
Russia	171 060 000	8 550 000
France	39 602 000	3 960 000
Italy	35 239 000	1 750 000
Serbia	2 912 000	291 000
Belgium	7 000 000	70 000
UK	45 370 000	2 268 000
Austria	49 210 000	4 921 000
Germany	64 926 000	6 493 000
Turkey	21 274 000	1 063 000

(a) For each country, calculate the percentage of the population
who were in the armed services.
(b) The table is divided into two parts. Calculate the percentage of
the total population of the countries in the top part who were
in the armed services.
(c) Do the same for the countries in the bottom part.
(d) Why is the table divided into two parts? (What was happening in 1915?)

4.2 A laboratory was testing a new drug for preventing a disease in animals. A number of new-born mice were divided into two groups. One group was given the new drug and the other was not. Both groups were placed in conditions where the disease was likely to be caught.

This table shows the results of the test.

	Caught disease	Did not catch disease	Total
Given drug	318	209	527
Not given drug	136	47	183
Total	454	256	710

Of the 454 mice who caught the disease, 318 had been given the drug. $\frac{318}{454} = 0{\cdot}70$ (to 2 d.p.) = 70%

A newspaper printed this story.

> **NEW DRUG IS USELESS**
>
> 70% of the mice who caught a disease had been given a new drug, according

Is this a fair conclusion to draw from the results of the test? Explain your answer.

5 Mappings

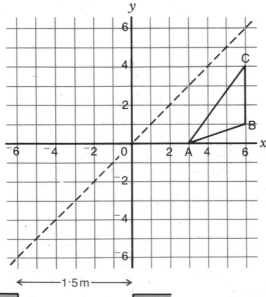

5.1 Draw this diagram.

(a) Reflect the triangle ABC in the li. $y = x$. Label the image A'B'C'.

(b) Reflect A'B'C' in the y-axis. Label the new image A"B"C".

(c) What single mapping will map triangle ABC onto triangle A"B"C

5.2 Draw the diagram again.

This time reflect ABC first in the y-axis and then reflect the result in the line $y = x$.

What single mapping will map the triangle ABC onto the final image?

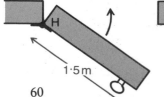

5.3 This drawing is a plan of a door which is supposed to rotate about the hinge H and fit snugly into the gap between the two walls. Will the door shut properly? If not, why not?

7 TV programmes survey

This activity is for a whole class working together.

A survey of TV programmes in the UK came up with these figures
for the percentage of broadcasting time given to different types of
programme.

Information	20·0%
Education	56·4%
Entertainment	15·5%
Programmes for specific audiences (children, religious groups, etc.)	8·1%

The survey was carried out before Channel 4 started and before
there was any TV at breakfast time.

In this chapter you will be carrying out small-scale surveys to find out
the percentage of time given to each kind of programme on a few
particular days. Of course, a few days may not be typical of a whole
year's broadcasting, so it would be wrong to draw any firm conclusions
from your results. But by doing a small-scale survey you will get some
idea of what is involved in larger surveys of this kind.

1 The next four pages contain information about the TV programmes
on all channels on a weekday.

Use this information to find what percentage of broadcasting time
is devoted to each of the four kinds of programme listed in the
table above. Do it for each channel separately, and also find the
overall percentages for all channels together.

'Information' includes news, documentaries, etc.
'Education' includes school and Open University broadcasts.
'Entertainment' includes drama, serials, films, quiz shows,
comedy, music, sports, etc.

Sometimes you will find it easy to decide whether a programme is
'information' or 'education' and so on. In other cases you might
find it difficult to decide. You may find programmes that are mixtures
of, say, information and entertainment, and you have to decide for
yourself what to do about them.

Write a brief report on your findings. Draw diagrams or charts to
illustrate them. Compare your findings with those of others.

BBC 1

6.30 BREAKFAST TIME presented by Frank Bough and Selina Scott

6.30	News, weather
6.37	Introducing the show's guests
6.43	Sports news, regional news
6.49	Safety at your barbecue
6.53	Keep fit
6.57	Weather

7.00	News
7.08	Motor-neurone disease: an interview with a doctor
7.12	Chat with guests
7.15	Regional news, sports news, travel news, weather
7.22	Security in your home
7.27	Chat
7.29	Weather

7.30	News
7.33	Chat
7.37	Gathering and selling cockles
7.41	Hetty, the injured tortoise who has had wheels fitted on her
7.45	News, weather
7.49	Pop news
7.54	Chat
7.57	Weather

8.00	News
8.08	Gold prospecting in California
8.11	Chat
8.15	Regional news, travel news, weather, sports news
8.20	Safety at motorcycle races
8.29	Weather

8.30	News
8.33	Review of today's papers
8.39	Your stars: horoscopes
8.44	Video quiz
8.49	Claire Rayner's advice on romance on holiday
8.52	Preview of today's TV
8.56	News, weather

9.00 FOR SCHOOLS AND COLLEGES

9.00	Lithography
9.30	Spanish conversation
9.48	Graphs
10.10	Episode eight of Fair Ground!
10.35	Religion and moral education
11.00	Watch
11.17	Walrus
11.40	Patterns in place
12.03	General studies

12.30 News after Noon

12.57 Regional news

1.00 Pebble Mill at One: a magazine programme of news stories, interviews and music

1.45 Fingerbobs. A See-Saw programme for the very young

2.00 You and me: for parents and children

2.15 FOR SCHOOLS AND COLLEGES

2.15	Words of Tomorrow
2.40	Cartoonists
3.00	Bernard Shaw lived here

3.15 Songs of Praise, from the church of St Mary Magdalene, Taunton

3.55 Play School. For the under-fives

4.20 Cartoon: Yogi Bear

4.25 Jackanory. Jana Sheldon reads part two of The Animal, the Vegetable and John D. Jones

4.40 Animal Magic: with John Morris and Terry Nutkins. The last programme in the series deals with the way animals navigate and highlights the programme's own homing pigeons

5.05 John Craven's Newsround

5.10 The Baker Street Boys: new series about a gang of street urchins who solve crimes in the manner of their Baker Street hero

5.40 News with Moira Stuart

6.00 South East at Six, presented by Laurie Mayer and Fran Morrison

6.25 **Nationwide,** with Richard Kershaw. A magazine programme of news stories and interviews

6.55 **Doctor Who.** Peter Davison in part three of Enlightenment

7.30 **Vox Pop.** Another programme in the documentary series that listens to the thoughts and words of some people of the small Lancashire town of Darwen

7.50 **Terry and June.** Comedy series

8.20 **Great Little Railways:** The Dragon of Sugar Island. Colin Garratt in the Philippines on a train that carries sugar cane to the mills

9.00 **News** with John Humphrys

9.25 **Play for Today: Gates of Gold,** by Maurice Leitch. The story of a mentally retarded 14-year old girl and the effect two travelling evangelists have on her.

10.35 **People and Power.** David Dimbleby with the weekly magazine programme on aspects of politics

11.18 **News** headlines

11.20 **World Figure Skating Championships** from Helsinki

11.55 **Weather**

11.57 Closedown

BBC 2

6.05 **OPEN UNIVERSITY**

    6.05 Modern Art – Monet
    6.30 Oceanography
    6.55 Cell Structure
    7.20 Into the Earth
    7.45 Seven Card Study
    8.10 Closedown

11.00 **Play School:** for the under-fives

11.25 Closedown

5.10 **Management and the School.** How a new headmaster persuades his staff and his pupils' parents to accept his ideas

5.40 **Manhunt of Mystery Island.** Part Two. Claire is captured by the evil Captain Mephisto

5.55 **Color Rhapsody.** The Columbia cartoon, Midnight Frolics

6.05 **The Bagthorpe Saga.** Comedy series about an eccentric family

6.30 **The Waltons.** John-Boy sorts out his professional career, while Rose, realising she has competition for Stanley's affections, goes on a crash diet

7.15 **News** summary with subtitles

7.20 **Film:** Silent Running (1971)

8.45 **The One That Gets Away.** Mountaineer Joe Brown goes fishing for trout at the bottom of a sheer 200-foot drop in one of Scotland's spectacular gorges

9.00 **Russell Harty.** Tonight he re-unites some show business personalities with their school teachers. Among those celebrities appearing are Toyah and Willie Rushton

9.30 **Arena: Kurt Vonnegut.** A documentary that traces the career of the controversial author

10.30 **Newsnight.** The latest world and domestic news plus an extended look at one of the main stories of the day

11.20 Interval

11.30 **OPEN UNIVERSITY**

    11.30 Telecommunications Networks
    11.55 Unemployment in the 1930's

12.25 Closedown

ITV

6.25 GOOD MORNING BRITAIN with
Anne Diamond and Martin Wainwright

6.25 Chat
6.28 Weather

6.30 News
6.35 Report on a new musical based on Wind in the Willows
6.39 Chat
6.40 Sports news
6.46 Chris Tarrant in Great Yarmouth: roller skating
6.52 Interview with head of a computer dating agency
6.58 Weather

7.00 News
7.05 Report on Shildon: a railway works about to close down
7.13 Preview of TV programmes
7.15 Introducing the show's guest
7.20 Chris Tarrant in Great Yarmouth. Chris talks to a snake handler and handles a snake himself
7.25 Competition time
7.28 Weather

7.30 News
7.33 Chris Tarrant talks to the manager of a circus
7.40 Sports news
7.47 Report on a Jehovah's Witness's attitude to blood transfusion
7.54 Pop Video time
7.59 Weather

8.00 News
8.05 Today's mystery guest
8.18 Chris Tarrant in Great Yarmouth: roller skating
8.25 Competition time
8.28 Weather

8.30 News
8.33 Cookery
8.40 Chris Tarrant talks to an actor
8.45 A handicapped child's wish come true

GOOD MORNING BRITAIN

8.50 Keep fit
8.55 Chat
8.57 Weather
9.00 News
9.05 Cartoon
9.15 Closedown

9.30 FOR SCHOOLS

9.30 Elementary arithmetic
9.45 Flight
10.04 Alive and kicking
10.21 The Electromagnetic Spectrum
10.43 Jonathan Dimbleby's The Eagle and the Bear
11.05 A history of the comic, Beano
11.22 Basic maths
11.39 French conversation

12.00 Cockleshell Bay. Adventures of the Cockle twins, for the very young
12.10 Once Upon a Time. Mark Wynter with the story of Little Red Riding Hood
12.30 The Sullivans: a serial
1.00 News
1.30 Crown Court. A man is accused of raping and killing a young girl after her younger brother identifies him as the man he saw on the common on the day of the murder
2.00 A plus presented by Trevor Hyett. Michael Straight discusses his book, After a Long Silence, with Nigel West
2.30 Love in a Cold Climate. Episode one of the Simon Raven adaptation of two Nancy Mitford novels
3.30 One of the Boys. Comedy series starring Mickey Rooney
4.00 Cockleshell Bay. A repeat of the programme shown at noon

| 4.15 | **The Moomins,** narrated by Richard Murdoch |

4.15 **The Moomins,** narrated by Richard Murdoch

4.20 **Stig of the Dump.** Stig helps Barney and Lon unravel the mystery of the Standing Stones

4.35 **Five Magic Minutes** with the Great Kovari

4.45 **CB TV – Channel 14.** News, views and ideas of young people

5.15 **Emmerdale Farm.** Jackie Merrick does Seth a favour and gets into trouble

5.45 **News**

6.00 **Regional News**

6.25 **Help!** With news for the ½ million pensioners who don't claim benefits they're entitled to

6.35 **Crossroads.** Sid Hooper is the recipient of some disappointing news

7.00 **Reporting London** presented by Michael Barratt. An investigation into the cause of the dwindling number of London Bingo halls.

7.35 **Film: Moonlight** (1982)

9.00 **Lifer.** A documentary by Rex Bloomstein about the conditions of people sentenced to life imprisonment

10.10 **News**

10.30 **Lifer** continued

11.30 **Lifer: A Live Studio Discussion**

12.15 Closedown

CHANNEL 4

4.45 **Years Ahead**: A magazine programme of interest to older viewers

5.30 **Wayne and Shuster.** This week the Canadian comics turn their attentions to the days of yore in Robin Hood Roast

6.00 **Mini Pops.** Children between the ages of seven and 10 imitate their musical heroes and heroines in a frantic half-an-hour of singing and dancing

6.30 **Common Interest: Enough is Enough.** An investigation into the plight of the poor in Coventry

7.00 **Channel Four News**

7.50 **Comment.** The nightly slot where people can air their grievances. Tonight it is the turn of union leader, Ken Gill

8.00 **Brookside.** Serial

8.30 **For What it's Worth.** Consumer affairs presented by David Stafford

9.00 **Eastern Eye** presented by Aziz Kurtha and Shyama Perera. There is a report from Birmingham on the new textile industry pioneered by Asians

10.00 **Film: Saint Jack** (1979)

12.05 Closedown

Categories

While you were carrying out your survey, you had to make decisions
about how to describe each programme. (Is it information or entertainment, etc.?)
Sometimes the decision is not clear. You may have decided to call a programme
'information' but someone else might call it 'entertainment'. How you decide
will affect the figures you end up with.

Look back at the table printed at the beginning of this chapter (page 61). In that
survey, as in your own, programmes were divided into four types or **categories**.
The people who carried out the survey had to decide, just as you did, which
category to put each programme into. If they had decided differently about
some programmes, the figures would have been different.

The four categories are not precise, because it is not always clear which
category a programme fits into. Because the categories are not precise, the
figures are not precise either. They are only a rough guide to the percentages
of different types of programme.

If there is a lot of room for disagreement about how to put things into
categories, then the results of a survey can be of little value. Here is an
example where this happened.
A local councillor who was in favour of school uniform was told by an
opponent that he was out of date, and that hardly any schools in the area
had school uniform. At the next council meeting, the first councillor produced
figures, 'the results of a survey of all schools in the area'.

Schools with a uniform	85%
Schools without a uniform	15%

But what does 'school uniform' mean? If a school has a school tie but
nothing else, does it count as having a school uniform? Some people would
say 'yes', others 'no'. The category 'schools with a uniform' is very imprecise,
so the figures do not mean much.

One way to get round the problem of imprecise categories in the case of the
TV survey is to have an extra category 'other types' for programmes which
will not fit into any of the main categories.

Further work

2   Get hold of information about one weekend's TV programmes.
Carry out a similar survey to your first one and write a brief
report comparing your findings for weekday and weekend
programmes.

3   Take 'sports' as a separate category of programme. Find the
percentage of weekend broadcasting time devoted to sports.

If all you have is ...

a pencil,
a pair of compasses, and
a straight edge,

you can bisect a line AB like this.

Set the compasses to a radius greater than $\frac{1}{2}$AB. With centre A draw two arcs on either side of AB.	With centre B and the same radius, draw arcs to cross the first two arcs.	Use the straight edge to draw a line through the points where the arcs cross.
	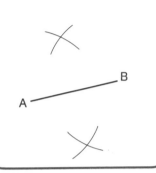	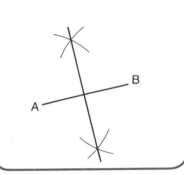

The line you have constructed is at right-angles to AB and cuts AB in half.
So it is called the **perpendicular bisector** of AB. ('Perpendicular' means 'at right-angles'.)

1 Draw a triangle ABC, of any size and shape.
   Construct the perpendicular bisectors of AB, of BC and of CA.
   What do you notice about them?

2 You are given a line, and a point P not on it.
   You have compasses and a straight edge.

   Show how to construct a line through P at
   right-angles to the given line.
   (The diagram shows a way of starting.)

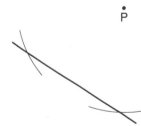

3 Draw a triangle ABC. Construct these three lines:
   (a) a line through A at right-angles to BC
   (b) a line through B at right-angles to AC
   (c) a line through C at right-angles to AB
   What do you notice about the three lines?

4 You are given a circle, but its centre is not marked.
   (a) P is a point on the circle. You have compasses and a straight edge.
       Show how to construct the diameter through P.
   (b) Show how to locate the centre of the circle.

5 Can you explain why the construction at the top of the page is correct?

8 Direct and inverse proportionality

A Direct proportionality

This diagram shows the cost of different lengths of lace edging.

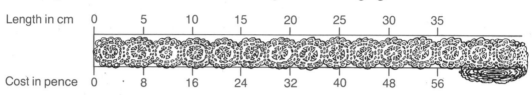

Length in cm	0	5	10	15	20	25	30	35

Cost in pence   0   ·   8   16   24   32   40   48   56

The cost of the edging is **proportional** to the length.
If you multiply the length by a number, say 3, then the
cost is multiplied by the same number.

×3

Length in cm	0	5	10	15	20	25	30	35
Cost in pence	0	8	16	24	32	40	48	56

×3

The graph of (length, cost) is a
straight line through $(0, 0)$.

The ratio $\dfrac{\text{cost in p}}{\text{length in cm}}$ is **constant**,
and is equal to the gradient of
the graph, which is $1 \cdot 6$.

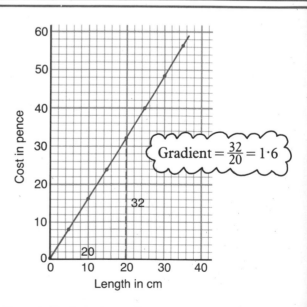

$$\text{Gradient} = \frac{32}{20} = 1 \cdot 6$$

A1 10 cm of the edging costs 16p. Calculate the cost of

    (a) 100 cm   (b) 300 cm   (c) 900 cm   (d) 8100 cm

If one variable q is proportional to another variable p, then these three things are true.

(1) The graph of (p, q) is a straight line through $(0, 0)$.

(2) **The multiplier rule**

If the value of p is multiplied by any number (e.g. 3), then the value of q is multiplied by the same number.

(3) **The constant ratio rule**

The ratio $\frac{q}{p}$ is the same for every pair of values of p and q, and is equal to the gradient of the graph of (p, q).

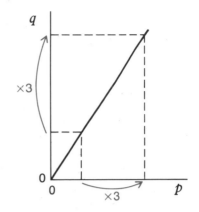

The multiplier rule and the constant ratio rule are both useful in calculations.

Worked example

The cost, C pence, of running an electric heater is proportional to the time, t hours, for which the heater is on.

If $C = 45$ when $t = 6 \cdot 5$, calculate
(a) t when $C = 167$ (b) C when $t = 150$

Set out the information in a table.

t	6·5	?	150
C	45	167	?

To show how to use both the multiplier rule and the constant ratio rule, we will use one rule to do (a) and the other to do (b). In fact, you can use either rule for either question.

(a)

t	6·5	a
C	45	167

The multiplier from 45 to 167 is $\frac{167}{45} = 3 \cdot 7 \ldots$

So multiply 6·5 by 3·7 . . . to get a. $a = 24 \cdot 1$, to 1 d.p.

(b)

t	6·5	150
C	45	b

The ratio $\frac{45}{6 \cdot 5}$ is $6 \cdot 9 \ldots$

So multiply 150 by 6·9 . . . to get b. $b = 1038 \cdot 5$, to 1 d.p.

A2   In an electroplating process, the mass m, in grams, of metal deposited is proportional to the time, t hours, for which the process runs.

If $m = 37 \cdot 5$ when $t = 5 \cdot 5$, calculate (to 1 d.p.)
(a) m when $t = 7 \cdot 5$ (b) t when $m = 100$

69

A3 If an object falls in a vacuum, its speed, v m/s, is proportional to the time, t seconds, since it was dropped.

If $v = 83·4$ when $t = 8·5$, calculate (to 1 d.p.)
(a) t when $v = 34·6$ (b) v when $t = 2·5$

A4 A variable q is proportional to another variable p.
When p is $17·3$, q is $6·3$.

Calculate (to 1 d.p.)
(a) q when p is $14·6$ (b) p when q is $8·2$ (c) p when q is $2·9$

B Inverse proportionality

B1 Mr Darby is organising a coach outing for his OAP club.
It costs £120 to hire the coach, which can take up to 40 people.

The amount he will have to charge will depend on the number of people who want to go. He is not out to make a profit; he just wants to break even.

Let p stand for the number of people who want to go.
Let c stand for the cost per person in £.

(a) Copy and complete this table of values of p and c.

p	2	3	4	6	10	20	30	40
c	60	40						

(b) What can you say about the product pc for every pair of values in the table?

(c) What happens to the value of c when the value of p is doubled?

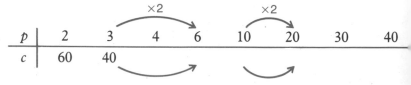

p	2	3	4	6	10	20	30	40
c	60	40						

(d) What happens to the value of c when the value of p is multiplied by 3?

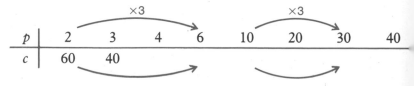

p	2	3	4	6	10	20	30	40
c	60	40						

(e) What happens to c when p is multiplied by 4?

For the two variables p and c in question B1, the product pc is constant, 120.

When the value of p is multiplied by a number, the value of c is **divided** by that number.

We say that c is **inversely proportional** to p.

The other kind of proportionality, dealt with in section A, is called **direct proportionality**.

Compare the two set of rules for direct and inverse proportionality.

Direct proportionality	Inverse proportionality
When one variable is multiplied by a number, the other is multiplied by the same number.	When one variable is multiplied by a number, the other is divided by the same number.
The ratio of the two variables is constant.	The product of the two variables is constant.

B2 The distance from Exeter to Liverpool is 240 miles.

(a) Suppose it is possible to travel all the way at a constant speed of 40 m.p.h. How long would the journey take?

(b) Copy and complete this table. s stands for speed in m.p.h. and t stands for the journey time in hours.

s	6	10	20	30	40	50	60	80	100	120
t										

(c) Is the product st constant?

(d) What happens to t when you multiply s by 3?

(e) Draw a graph of (s, t). Suitable scales are shown on the right.

(The curve is called a rectangular hyperbola.)

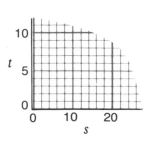

B3 Boyle's law says that provided the temperature does not change the volume of a gas is inversely proportional to its pressure.

Let V be the volume in litres, and P the pressure in millibars.

(a) If V is 18 when P is 800, calculate V when P is 1200, like this:

(i) Find the multiplier from 800 to 1200.

(ii) **Divide** by this number to find the new value of V.

P	800	1200
V	18	

(b) If V is 30 when P is 1800, calculate V when P is (i) 2250 (ii) 4050

71

Mathematics and music

When a guitar string is plucked, it produces a musical note which may be a high note or a low note. The highness or lowness depends on the **frequency** with which the string vibrates.

Frequency is measured in **hertz** (Hz). A string which vibrates 200 times per second produces a note whose frequency is **200 Hz**.

High notes have high frequencies and low notes low frequencies.

The frequency of the note produced by each string on a guitar depends on how tight the string is, and on the length of the vibrating part of the string.

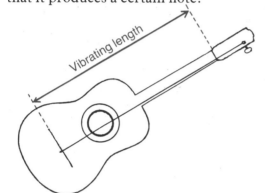

Before starting to play, the guitar player adjusts the tightness of each string so that it produces a certain note.

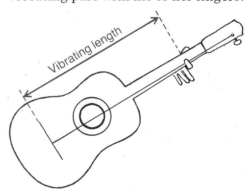

The player gets higher notes from the same string by altering the length of the vibrating part with his or her fingers.

If the vibrating length is divided by 2, the frequency doubles (and we hear the note 'an octave higher'). In fact, the frequency of the note is **inversely proportional** to the length of the vibrating string.

Worked example

A string of length 70 cm has been 'tuned' to produce a note whose frequency is 110 Hz. Calculate the length which will produce a note of frequency 185 Hz.

First we work out the multiplier from 110 Hz to 185 Hz.

It is $\frac{185}{110} = 1 \cdot 68 \ldots$

The length is inversely proportional to the frequency. So if the frequency is multiplied by 1·68, the length has to be **divided** by 1·68.

So the length has to be $\frac{70 \, \text{cm}}{1 \cdot 68 \ldots} = 41 \cdot 6 \, \text{cm}$

(to 3 s.f.)

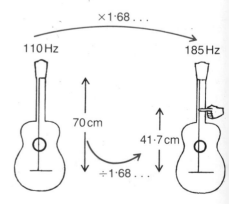

B4 A string of length 65 cm has been tuned to produce a note whose frequency is 150 Hz. Calculate the length which will produce a note of frequency 175 Hz.

B5 The note whose frequency is 110 Hz is called A. The second lowest string on a guitar is tuned to this note.

Here are the frequencies of some other notes which can be produced from the A-string, by altering the length.

Note	B	C	D	E	F	G
Frequency	124	131	147	165	175	196

If the vibrating A-string (110 Hz) is 70 cm long, calculate the length needed to produce each of the notes in the table.

B6 Another string on a guitar is tuned to the note D (147 Hz). If this string is 70 cm long, calculate the length of it which will produce the note G (196 Hz).

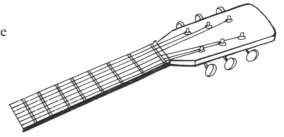

On a guitar there are 'frets' which enable the player to get the right length of string for each note.

The spacing of these frets is worked out from calculations like those you have just done in questions B5 and B6.

~Facts about frequencies

This diagram shows the frequencies of some of the notes on a piano. (They are all As).

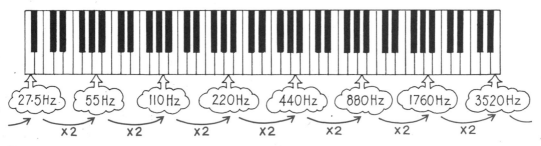

The range of frequencies which can be heard by human beings extends from about 15 Hz to 20 000 Hz, but the upper limit comes down as people get older. Dogs and cats can hear frequencies up to 60 000 Hz, and bats up to 80 000 Hz.

You can also do inverse proportionality calculations by using the 'constant product' rule.

Worked example

q is inversely proportional to p, and q is 4·6 when p is 3·5.
Calculate   (a) q when p is 2·5   (b) p when q is 1·7.

First make a table.

p	3·5	2·5	b
q	4·6	a	1·7

To find the constant product, do $3·5 \times 4·6 = 16·1$.

(a) The product of 2·5 and a must also be 16·1.

So $2·5a = 16·1$.

$$a = \frac{16·1}{2·5} = 6·4 \text{ to 1 d.p.}$$

(b) $1·7b = 16·1$

$$b = \frac{16·1}{1·7} = 9·5 \text{ to 1 d.p.}$$

B7 The frequency, f Hz, of a radio wave is inversely proportional to the wavelength, w m.

When w is 1350, f is 222. Calculate, to 3 s.f.,
(a) f when $w = 800$ (b) w when $f = 1000$ (c) f when $w = 1850$

B8 q is inversely proportional to p, and q is 0·62 when p is 4·85.
Calculate   (a) q when p is 0·62   (b) p when q is 4·85

*B9 The time T minutes taken to cook a piece of meat in a microwave oven is directly proportional to the weight W kg of the meat and inversely proportional to the power setting P watts.

It takes 6 minutes to cook a piece of meat weighing 1·2 kg on a power setting of 500 watts. How long will it take to cook a piece weighing 3·0 kg on a power setting of 800 watts?

*B10 (a) A variable Y is **directly** proportional to another variable X. What is the percentage change (increase or decrease) in Y when X is

(i) increased by 20%   (ii) decreased by 20%

(b) A variable V is inversely proportional to another variable U. What is the percentage change (increase or decrease) in V when U is

(i) increased by 20%   (ii) decreased by 20%

9 Representing information

1S	1E	1S	3W	1E	1E	3S
1E	1N	1E	1N	1S	2S	1N
1N	1E	1E	★	1E	2W	1S
1S	1N	2E	1N	2N	2W	3N
2N	1W	1N	3E	1W	1E	5W

This is a puzzle. You have to start on one of the coloured squares and find a path to the centre. Each square is marked with an instruction, telling you which square to move to next.

For example, if you land on the square in the top right-hand corner, marked '3S', you must go 3 squares south. So the next square you land on will be the one marked '3N'.

A1 Only one of the coloured squares will lead you to the centre. Which one is it?

A2 How many squares can you find where if you start there and follow the instructions, you get back to where you started?

Most people start by trying to solve the puzzles by trial and error.
You could find the path to the centre by trying out each coloured square
in turn until you find the right one.

Another way to find the path to the centre is to start there and
work backwards.

When you come to the second puzzle (squares which you get back to) then
trial and error is a very long-winded method. A much better method is
to **represent the information differently**, like this.

1   Put a piece of tracing paper over the diagram. Mark a dot
in each square.

Represent each instruction by an arrow showing where to go from
that square. **Do this square by square across the diagram; do not
go from square to square along the arrows.**
This diagram shows the arrows from the squares in the top row.

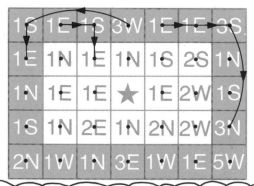

Turn back to the previous page. On tracing paper, complete the
diagram showing all the arrows, before you read on.

2   Here is the finished diagram. This kind of diagram with dots
joined by arrows is called a **network**.

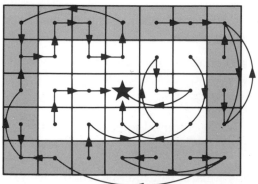

From this diagram you can solve both puzzles easily.

A3 Either put a piece of tracing paper over the diagram below or copy it on squared paper.

Draw a network with arrows representing the instructions.

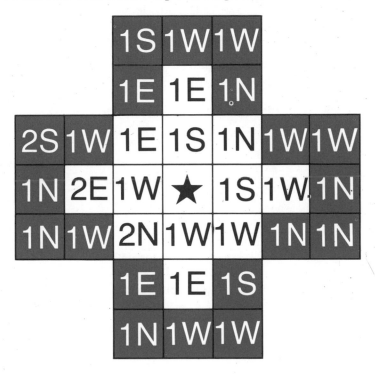

(a) Which coloured square leads to the centre?

(b) How many closed loops are there in the network?
(A closed loop is a path which leads back to where it started.)

A4 This is a different kind of puzzle.
There are six people: A, B, C, D, E and F.

Not everyone knows everyone else. These pairs know each other:

A and B	A and C	A and D	A and E
A and F	B and D	C and E	D and F

The six people have to sit in a row, so that nobody is next to a person they don't know.

Find a way to seat them. How many different ways can you find?

If you didn't have to worry about who knows who, but just had to seat six people in a row, there are lots of ways to do it (720 in fact).

Trying out each one to see if it solves the puzzle would take a long time! Once again a network helps to solve the puzzle.

1 Represent each person by a dot.

Whenever two people know one another, join their two dots.

For example, A and F know one another.

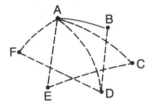

2 Here is the complete network. There are no arrows this time, because each connection works both ways: if A knows F then F knows A. (You could put arrows pointing both ways on each line →←.)

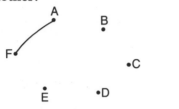

3 Try starting with A. A knows B, so we could put B next, ... and B knows D, so D could come next, ... and D knows F, . . .

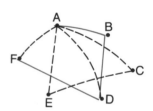

4 But then who? The only other line from F returns to A, so there is nobody left who can sit next to F!

What we need is a **tour** – a route through the network which visits every dot just once.

5 For example, we could go CEAFDB, or in reverse order BDFAEC.
These are not the only solutions. Counting reversals there are 8 solutions altogether.

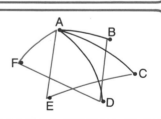

A5 Copy the network. Find as many as you can of the other 6 solutions to the puzzle.
Write down the sequence of letters in each case.

A6 There are five people: A, B, C, D and E.
These pairs know one another: A, C   A, D   B, C   C, D   D, E

(a) Draw a network to represent this information.

(b) Find a way to stand the five people in a line so that nobody is next to a stranger.

(c) How many different ways are there to do it?

(d) Which two people must stand at the ends of the line?

(e) The five people are joined by an extra person F who knows only A. In how many ways can all six people stand in line with nobody next to a stranger? Explain your answer.

A7 Two words are 'friendly' if they have only one letter different. For example, SOUR is friendly with HOUR, SPUR, SOAR, SOUL, etc.

In a 'word chain' each word is friendly with the next.
For example, here is how to change BEER into WINE:

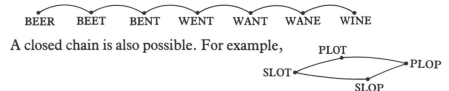

BEER   BEET   BENT   WENT   WANT   WANE   WINE

A closed chain is also possible. For example,

PLOT
SLOT   PLOP
SLOP

(a) Draw a network with eight dots for these words:
FLAT   SLAG   SLIT   SLAB   FLAB   SLAT   FLAG   FLIT

Connect the dots whenever two words are friendly.

(b) Find two different ways to connect the words in a closed chain.

A8 Seven people, A, B, C, D, E, F and G are going for a meal together. They have to sit round a circular table.

The following pairs know one another.
A, B   A, C   A, D   A, E   A, F   A, G   B, C
C, D   C, F   C, G   D, E   D, G   F, G

Find out how the seven people can sit round the table so that each person knows the two people on either side of them.

B   Two-way tables

B1 The 116 children in the first year of a school were asked if they liked or disliked maths.
39 children said they disliked it.
48 of the girls said they liked it.
There were 57 boys altogether. How many of them said they disliked maths?

A two-way table is a useful way of representing the information given in question B1.

The children can be split up into girls and boys (nobody is both).
They can also be split up into those who like maths and those who do not.

One of these ways of splitting up is used to label the rows of a table and the other is used to label the columns.

This table shows the numbers we know. It is now easy to work out the missing numbers.

	Like maths	Dislike maths	Total
Girls	48		
Boys			57
Total		39	116

B2 There are 326 children in a school.
94 children wear glasses, of whom 55 are boys.
125 girls do not wear glasses.

(a) Make a two-way table and fill in all the numbers in it.

(b) How many boys are there in the school?

B3 A car factory turned out 582 cars in a week, 109 of them having left-hand drive. Metallic paint was used on 267 cars altogether. 288 of the right-hand drive cars were painted with non-metallic paint.

Make a two-way table and work out how many of the left-hand drive cars were painted with metallic paint.

B4 In a school of 519 pupils, 146 study both French and German. Altogether 385 pupils study French and 271 study German.

(a) One boy started to make a two-way table like this.
Why is it wrong?

	French	German	Total

(b) Make a two-way table correctly.

(c) How many pupils study neither of the two languages?

B5 Here is some of the information obtained from a survey of coffee drinkers.
65% took sugar.
75% took milk.
45% took both.

What percentage took neither sugar nor milk?

B6 15% of the members of a tennis club are men aged 30 or over, and 37% are women aged under 30. Altogether 61% of the members are under 30. What percentage of the members are women?

c Network tables

A network and a table of numbers look like two entirely different kinds
of thing. However, the information in a network can be written in the
form of a two-way table, as you will find from the next questions.

(By means of a table, the information in a network can be stored in
a computer.)

C1   Here is a network, ... and here is a table, not yet finished.

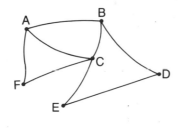

	A	B	C	D	E	F
A	0	1	1	0	0	1
B	1	0	1	1	0	0
C	1	1	0	0	1	1
D						
E						
F						

(a) Look at the vertex A in the network and then look at row A
in the table. Why is there a 1 under B, C and F, but a 0 under
A, D and E?

(b) In row B of the table, why is there a 1 under A, C and D, but
a 0 under B, E and F?

(c) Copy the table and fill in the rows D, E and F.

C2   Make a similar table for each of these networks.

(a)   (b)   (c)

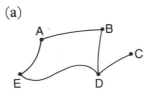

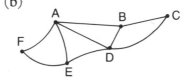

C3   Draw a network from the
information in each of
these tables.

(a)

	A	B	C
A	0	1	0
B	1	0	1
C	0	1	0

(b)

	A	B	C	D
A	0	0	1	1
B	0	0	1	1
C	1	1	0	1
D	1	1	1	0

The lines going from vertex to vertex in a network are called **edges**.
The network in question C1 has 8 edges: AB, AC, AF, BC, BD, CE, CF, DE.

C4   For each network and table you have got so far (in C1, C2 and C3), find
(i) the number of edges in the network
(ii) the total of all the numbers in the table
What do you notice? Explain it.

C5 In this network there is more than one edge between some pairs of vertices, . . .

. . . and the numbers are shown in the table.

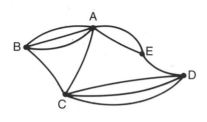

	A	B	C	D	E
A	0	3	1	0	2
B					
C					
D					
E					

(a) Copy and complete the table.

(b) Is the rule you found in question C4 still true?

C6 A **complete** network is one in which every vertex is joined up to every other one by an edge.

This is a complete network with 5 vertices, together with its table.

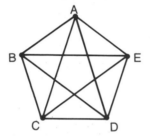

	A	B	C	D	E
A	0	1	1	1	1
B	1	0	1	1	1
C	1	1	0	1	1
D	1	1	1	0	1
E	1	1	1	1	0

(a) From the numbers in the table, calculate the number of edges in the network.

(b) Make a table for a complete network with 6 vertices. Do not draw the network.

Calculate the number of edges in the network.

(c) Imagine the table for a complete network with 7 vertices. Calculate the number of edges in the network.

(d) Calculate the number of edges in a complete network with

(i) 10 vertices   (ii) 20 vertices   (iii) 100 vertices

(e) Imagine the table for a complete network with n vertices. How many rows and columns will it have?
What does each row have in it? What is the total of each row? What is the total of all the rows?

Write an expression for the number of edges in the network.

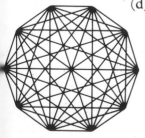

Algebra review (2)

1 Solve each of these equations.

   (a) $3x + 10 = x + 26$ (b) $2x - 30 = 3x - 5$

   (c) $6x - 2 = 3x + 19$ (d) $5 - 4x = 7x - 28$

2 Multiply out the brackets in these expressions and simplify.

   (a) $3a + 2(a + 4)$ (b) $5b - 3(b + 1)$ (c) $10c - 4(3 + 2c)$

   (d) $14 - 3(4 - 3d)$ (e) $8e - 5(3 - 2e)$ (f) $7 - 4(2f + 3)$

3 Factorise each of these expressions. The first is done as an example.

   (a) $3a^2 + 6ab = 3a(a + 2b)$ (b) $4b + 6bc$ (c) $8c^2 + 10c$

   (d) $6d - 15d^2$ (e) $12 - 8e^2$ (f) $6fg - 8g^2$ (g) $30g - 4g^2$

4 The dimensions of a cuboid are
a cm, b cm and c cm.

  Write down an expression, in its
simplest form, for

   (a) the total length in cm of all the edges

   (b) the total area in cm^2 of all the faces

   (c) the volume in cm^3

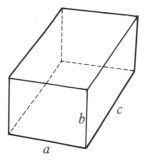

5 Two classes collect money for charity. In the first class
a children collect a total of £x. In the second class
b children collect a total of £y.

  Write down an expression for

   (a) the mean amount collected per child in the first class

   (b) the mean amount collected per child in the second class

   (c) the overall mean amount per child for the two classes together

6 Make the letter printed in red the subject of each formula.

   (a) $s = ar - t$ (b) $s = ar - t$ (c) $g = \dfrac{m}{a} + n$

   (d) $t = \dfrac{ax}{by}$ (e) $t = \dfrac{ax}{by}$ (f) $b = \dfrac{h}{a + x}$

10 Looking at data

A The median of a set of measurements

The word **data** means information, usually in the form of numbers.

The data below consists of the weights in kg of the 15 boys in a rugby team.

48 56 50 65 47 63 71 60 52 42 61 58 45 67 53

We can see how the weights are spread out by marking them on a scale.
In the diagram below, the boys are numbered 1 to 15 in order of weight,
starting with the lightest.

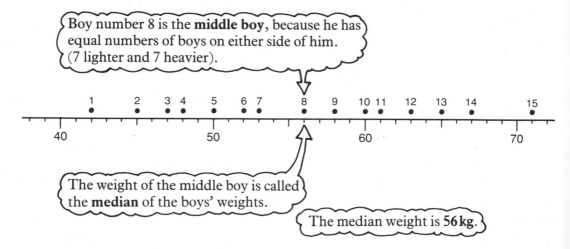

Boy number 8 is the **middle boy**, because he has equal numbers of boys on either side of him. (7 lighter and 7 heavier).

The weight of the middle boy is called the **median** of the boys' weights.

The median weight is **56 kg**.

A useful way of summarising data is to give

> the smallest value
> the median value
> the largest value
> the range (the difference between the smallest and largest values)

So we can summarise the data above like this:

Smallest 42 kg Median 56 kg Largest 71 kg Range 29 kg

A1 Here are the weights in kg of the 11 girls in a hockey team.

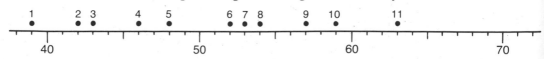

(a) Which number girl is the middle girl?
(b) Summarise the data by giving the smallest, median, largest
and range.

A2 Here are the heights in metres of 23 trees in a plantation.

(a) If the trees are numbered in order of height from 1 to 23, smallest first, which number is the middle one?

(b) Summarise the data as before.

When there is an even number of measurements in the set, then there is no 'middle one'.

For example here are the weights in kg of 10 children. There is no single 'middle child', but children numbers 5 and 6 form a 'middle pair'. There are equal numbers of children on either side of the middle pair.

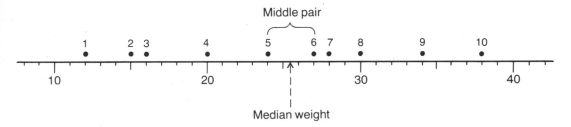

The median weight is taken to be halfway between the weights of the middle pair. So in this case the median weight is **25·5 kg**.

A3 Here are the heights in cm of 16 girls.

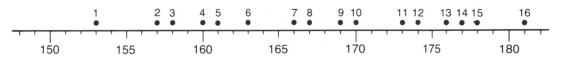

(a) Which number girls form the middle pair?

(b) What is the median of the girls' heights?

A4 Finding the 'middle one' or the 'middle pair'

(a) In a group of 8, the middle pair is 4, 5.

1   2   3   (4   5)   6   7   8

What is the middle pair in a group of 14?

Find a rule for working out the numbers of the middle pair when there is an even number in the group.

(b) Find a rule for working out the number of the middle one when there is an odd number in the group.

The diagram below shows the weights of 24 new-born babies, in kg. Some babies have the same weight. But the babies are still numbered from 1 to 24 in order of weight.

Babies numbers 12 and 13 are the middle pair. They both weigh 3·6 kg, so 3·6 kg is the median weight.

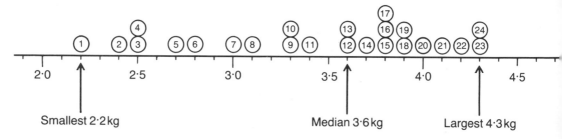

The spacing of the smallest, median and largest tells us something about the data.

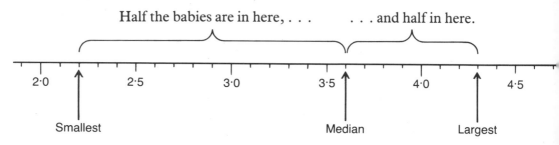

A5 Summarise the data given below by giving the smallest value, the median, the largest value and the range.

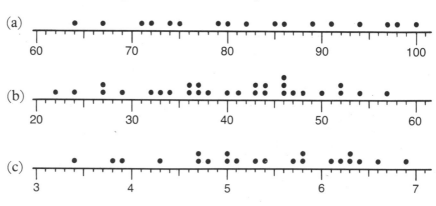

A6 These are the waist measurements, in cm, of 25 boys.

74 76 70 70 73 70 73 64 57 76 72 72 85
76 81 76 61 69 67 88 76 82 63 78 72

Summarise the data, as before.

86

B Stem-and-leaf tables

Here are the marks gained by 27 pupils in an examination.

```
73  48  71  62  69  75  79  85  80  64
67  73  86  91  54  78  69  50  75  84
90  54  57  43  80  91  78
```

One way to see this data as a whole is to show the marks as dots on a 'scale'.
Another way is to make a **stem-and-leaf** table, like this.

First we notice that the first figures (the tens figures) of the marks go from 4 up to 9.

We write these tens figures in the left-hand column of a table. These are the 'stems'.

```
4|
5|
6|
7|
8|
9|
```

Then we go through the marks one by one, and put the units figure of each mark in the proper row. These are the 'leaves'.

First 73,   then 48,   then 71, . . .

```
4|         4|8        4|8
5|         5|         5|
6|         6|         6|
7|3        7|3        7|31
8|         8|         8|
9|         9|         9|
```

When all the marks are entered, the table looks like this.

```
4|8 3
5|4 0 4 7
6|2 9 4 7 9
7|3 1 5 9 3 8 5 8
8|5 0 6 4 0
9|1 0 1
```

Now we re-write the table so that the units figures in each row are in order of size, smallest first.

```
4|3 8
5|0 4 4 7
6|2 4 7 9 9
7|1 3 3 5 5 8 8 9
8|0 0 4 5 6
9|0 1 1
```

This is a stem-and-leaf table.

The stem-and-leaf table is itself a kind of frequency chart. We can see from it that, for example, there are 2 pupils in the 40–49 group.
The **modal group** (the one with the highest frequency) is the 70–79 group.

In one way the table is better than a frequency bar chart, because the original data can still be seen. So we can use the table to find the median.

There are 27 pupils, so the middle one is number 14, counting up from the one with the lowest mark. From the table we can see that the lowest mark is 43, the next is 48, the next 50, and so on.

B1 What is the median mark in the table?

B2 These are exam marks of 15 pupils.

$$64 \quad 76 \quad 48 \quad 53 \quad 68 \quad 56 \quad 74 \quad 60$$
$$53 \quad 61 \quad 83 \quad 67 \quad 64 \quad 55 \quad 45$$

(a) Make a stem-and-leaf table of the marks.

(b) Which is the modal group?

(c) Find the median mark.

(d) What is the range of the marks?

B3 These are the weights, in kilograms, of 20 new-born babies.

$$2{\cdot}5 \quad 2{\cdot}8 \quad 3{\cdot}3 \quad 2{\cdot}6 \quad 3{\cdot}0 \quad 1{\cdot}8 \quad 3{\cdot}6 \quad 4{\cdot}0$$

$$2{\cdot}8 \quad 4{\cdot}1 \quad 1{\cdot}6 \quad 4{\cdot}3 \quad 3{\cdot}9 \quad 2{\cdot}5 \quad 3{\cdot}0 \quad 2{\cdot}3$$

$$4{\cdot}1 \quad 2{\cdot}7 \quad 4{\cdot}2 \quad 3{\cdot}5$$

(a) This time the units figure will be the 'stem' and the first decimal place the 'leaf'. Make a stem-and-leaf table with its left-hand column like this:

```
1·│
2·│
3·│
4·│
```

(b) Find the median weight of the babies.

B4 A group of pupils took two examination papers in maths, paper 1 and paper 2. Here are stem-and-leaf tables of the marks in the two papers.

Paper 1		**Paper 2**	
2	3 5 5	2	0 0 1 4 7
3	0 4 5 7	3	1 1 4 4 5 7 8
4	0 3 4 6 9	4	2 2 5 5 5 8 8 9
5	2 2 5 7	5	0 2 2 5 6 7
6	1 3 5 5 6 8	6	1 3 4 4 9 9
7	0 1 4 4 6 8 9	7	0 2 2 5
8	0 2 3 3 6 7 7	8	3 6 9
9	1 1 3 4 5	9	1 4

(a) Which paper was harder on the whole? How can you tell?

(b) Find the median mark for each paper.

(c) Find the range of marks for each paper.

Comparing two sets of data

Medians are often used when two sets of data are being compared. Here is an example of this.

The lengths of some male and female slow-worms were measured in cm. (A slow-worm looks like a snake but is in fact a legless lizard.)

The lengths are marked on these two scales, together with the median length for each sex.

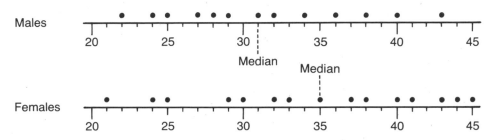

The median male length is 31 cm. The males are grouped around 31 cm with equal numbers on either side of 31 cm.

The median female length is 35 cm. The females are grouped around 35 cm with equal numbers on either side of 35 cm.

The fact that the median female length is greater than the median male length shows that as a group the females are longer than the males. Although half of the females are 35 cm or more, less than half of the males are 35 cm or more.

The fact that the **range** of the female lengths is greater than that of the male length shows that the females are more widely spread out in length.

The experiment described in the next question is typical of many experiments in which two sets of data have to be compared.

B5 A biologist wanted to compare the lengths of worms found living in two different kinds of soil. She collected some worms from each kind of soil and measured their lengths (unstretched). Here are the lengths in millimetres.

Soil A 38 47 43 51 45
33 62 57 36 40
49 66 55 49 45
31 40 44 57 58
35 52 73 39 38
69 46 55

Soil B 48 52 54 37 42
65 70 49 61 50
54 45 61 72 74
64 56 38 65 69
71 67 71 70 68

(a) Make a stem-and-leaf table for each group of worms.

(b) Find the shortest, median, longest and range for each group.

(c) Write a brief report comparing the two groups of worms.

C Averages: median and mean

The word 'average' has rather a vague meaning when used in everyday life.
It means 'not very large, not very small, somewhere about the middle'.
A man of 'average height' is neither particularly tall nor particularly short.

When people talk about the average of a set of numbers or measurements,
they are usually referring to the **mean**. But the **median** is often used as an
average value instead of the mean. The next question illustrates this.

C1 A company employs 40 people. Their monthly earnings in £ are listed
below in order of size, starting with the least well-paid.

250	250	250	260	260	270	280	280	280	290
290	300	300	310	320	320	320	320	330	330
330	340	340	350	350	350	380	380	390	390
390	740	860	920	1120	1280	1460	1710	1920	2070

(a) What is the median of the employees' monthly earnings?

(b) The total of all 40 employees' monthly earnings is £21880.
(You can check this if you like.) Calculate the mean of the
employees' monthly earnings.

(c) Which value, the mean or the median, gives a better idea of
the 'average' monthly earnings in the company?

(d) Which 'average' – median or mean – would you quote if you were
a union leader putting forward a claim for higher pay?

(e) Which would you quote if you were the managing director?

(f) If the mean is used as the average, how many of the 40
employees have 'above average' monthly earnings?

In the example in the previous question, the mean is high because of the
high earnings of a few employees. If these few were paid even more
the mean would increase, but the median would remain the same.

C2 20 batteries of a particular make were tested by connecting each one
to a bulb and seeing how long the battery lasted. The lifetimes
of the batteries, in hours, are given below in order of length,
shortest first.

3	4	6	6	7	18	29	33
34	34	35	37	37	37	39	40
40	41	42	42				

(a) What is the median of the batteries' lifetimes?

(b) Calculate the mean lifetime of the 20 batteries.

(c) Which value, median or mean, gives a better idea of the
'average' lifetime?

If all you have is ...
a pencil, and
a strip with parallel edges (a ruler
will do, if you ignore the markings),

you can construct a right-angle like this.

Use the strip to draw a pair of parallel lines.	Draw another pair across the first two.	Draw lines through the points of intersection. These lines cross at right-angles.
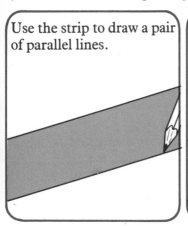	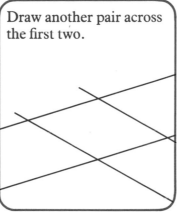	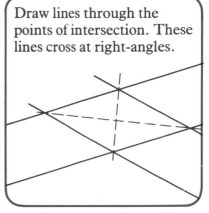

The dotted lines cross at right-angles because they are the diagonals
of a rhombus. But how do we know the shape is a rhombus?
It is certainly a parallelogram because opposite sides are parallel,
but we need to be sure that the sides are all equal.

1   Let d be the distance between the parallel
    lines in each pair.
    Let a and b be the lengths of the sides of
    the parallelogram.

    The area of the parallelogram can be
    found in two ways: either a or b can
    be thought of as the base. Use this to
    explain why a and b must be equal.

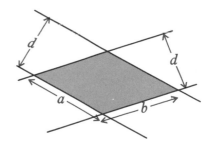

Show how to do each of the following constructions using only a
pencil and a strip with parallel edges.

2   Bisect a given angle.

3   Draw the perpendicular bisector of a line whose length
    is greater than the width of the strip.

4   Extend a given line to twice its length.

5   Given a line l and a point P on it, draw a line through P
    at right-angles to l.

6   Given a square, draw a square of double the area.

7   Draw the perpendicular bisector of a line whose length is
    less than the width of the strip.

11 Percentage (2)

A Percentages of percentages

Imagine a machine whose output is
80% of its input.
So if the input is P, the output is
80% of P or $0.8P$.
The machine is a $\times 0.8$ machine.

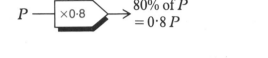

Now link this machine to another,
whose output is 60% of its input.
The second machine is a $\times 0.6$
machine.

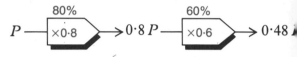

The final output is $0.8P \times 0.6 = 0.48P$.
So the two machines together do the
job of a $\times 0.48$ machine, and the
final output is 48% of the original
input.

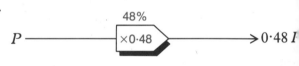

A1 A machine whose output is 30% of its input is linked to
another whose output is 70% of its input.
What percentage of the original input is the final output?

A2 A machine whose output is 40% of its input is linked to
another identical machine.
What percentage of the original input is the final output?

Traffic flows

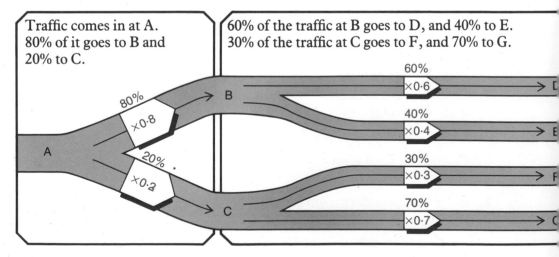

Traffic comes in at A.
80% of it goes to B and
20% to C.

60% of the traffic at B goes to D, and 40% to E.
30% of the traffic at C goes to F, and 70% to G.

A3 Let P stand for the amount of traffic coming in at A.

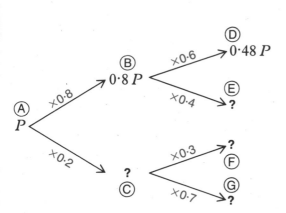

(a) Copy and complete this branching diagram to show the amounts at B, C, D, E, F and G.

Branching diagrams are usually called **tree diagrams**, even though trees generally branch upwards.

(b) 48% of the traffic coming in at A gets to D.
What percentage of the traffic at A gets to   (i) E   (ii) F   (iii) G

(c) Check that the percentages of traffic at D, E, F and G add up to 100%.

A4 60% of the population of a village are male and 40% are female.
80% of the males are under 65, and 20% are over 65 (65 or over).
70% of the females are under 65, and 30% are over 65.

This information is shown in the tree diagram on the right.
P stands for the total population of the village. Each percentage has been replaced by its decimal equivalent.

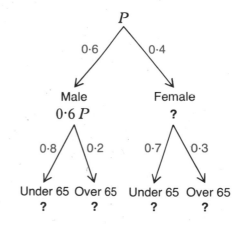

(a) Copy and complete the diagram.

(b) What percentage of the total population is in each of the four subgroups?

(c) What percentage of the total population is under 65 (regardless of sex)?

A5 35% of the students at a college wear glasses.
45% of those who wear glasses are men.
60% of those who do not wear glasses are men.

(a) Let P stand for the total number of students. Draw a tree diagram whose first branching shows 'wearing glasses' and 'not wearing glasses' and whose second branching shows 'men' and 'women'.

(b) Calculate the percentage of the students in each of the four subgroups.

A6 28% of the newts in a lake are male. 66% of the males and 52% of the females are over 10 cm long. What percentage of the newts are under 10 cm long?

B Percentage increases and decreases

Suppose rail fares go up by 18%.
This means that the increase added on
to the old fare is 18% of the old fare.

So the new fare is altogether 118% of
the old.

The decimal equivalent of 118% is
1·18. So the new fare is 1·18 times
the old fare.

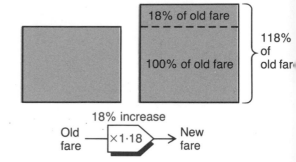

B1 What do you multiply the old fare by to get the new fare
when fares go up by
(a) 25%   (b) 13%   (c) 20%   (d) 8%   (e) 16·5%

Suppose fares go up twice in one year. The first time they go up by 23%,
and the second time by 9%.
The multiplier for the first increase is 1·23 and for the second 1·09,
as shown in this diagram.

Altogether, the old fare is multiplied by 1·23 × 1·09 = 1·3407.
A multiplier of 1·3407 means a percentage increase of **34·07%**,
so this is the overall percentage increase.

B2 Calculate the overall percentage increase for each of these.
(a) A 30% increase followed by a 40% increase
(b) A 40% increase followed by a 30% increase
(c) An 8% increase followed by a 12·5% increase
(d) Two successive increases of 20%

Suppose fares go down by 23%.
This means that 23% is subtracted
from the old fare, leaving 77%.

So the new fare is 0·77 times the
old fare.

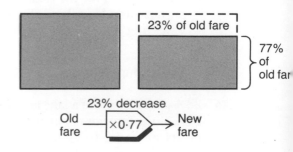

B3 What do you multiply the old fare by to get the new fare
when fares go down by
(a) 14%   (b) 7%   (c) 22%   (d) 24·5%   (e) 3·5%

B4 Calculate the overall percentage decrease for each of these.
(a) A 20% decrease followed by a 30% decrease
(b) A 16% decrease followed by a 9% decrease
(c) Two successive decreases of 11%

B5 House prices rose by 15% in the first half of a year and then
fell by 8% in the second half.

(c) Calculate the overall percentage increase or decrease.

B6 In 1981, the Greater London Council reduced fares on London
Transport by 30%. This reduction was later declared illegal, and
fares were doubled in 1982. In 1983, the fares were reduced by 25%.

Calculate the overall percentage increase or decrease in fares
between 1981 and 1983.

B7 Lord Snooty wants to increase the admission charge to his stately
home by 30%. His accountant thinks that doing this will reduce
the number of visitors by 25%. If the accountant is right, what
will be the percentage increase or decrease in the takings from visitors?

Interest

If you invest some money in a building society or a bank deposit account,
the money earns **interest**. You are being paid by the building society or
bank to lend them your money.

If the interest rate is, say, 8% per year, then your money increases by 8%
every year, and we say the **annual interest rate** is 8%. Instead of
'per year' we often say 'per annum'. ('Annum' comes from the Latin word
for 'year'.)

This diagram shows what happens to your money if the annual interest
rate is 8% and you leave the money in the bank or building society
for several years.

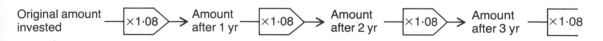

B8 If you invest £50 in a building society and the interest rate is 6% p.a. (per annum), how much do you have, to the nearest penny, after
    (a) 1 year   (b) 2 years   (c) 3 years   (d) 4 years   (e) 5 years

The instructions for calculating the yearly amounts, in question B8, can be written in the form of a diagram, called a **flow chart**.

The loop in the chart shows that the same thing is done again and again.

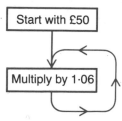

Flow charts are often used to give people precise instructions on how to carry out a certain type of calculation. They are also used by computer programmers, who need to break down a complicated calculation into simpler steps.

The flow chart shown above is not much use, because it does not say anything about how many years have been counted, and it does not say anything about when to stop.

Suppose we want to calculate the amount after 5 years. Then this flow chart tells us precisely what to do.

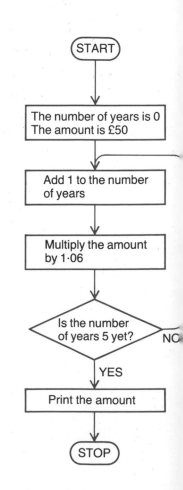

The start of the flow chart is clearly shown.

There are two quantities we have to deal with, the number of years and the amount of money.

To start with the number of years is 0, and the amount is £50.

We add 1 to the number of years, . . .

. . . and multiply the amount by 1·06.

The diamond shaped box is a 'question box'. It asks 'Is the number of years equal to 5 yet?' Which way we go next depends on the answer. If it is 'no' we go round the loop, . . .

If 'yes' we go on to print out the amount, . . .

. . . and stop.

B9 You invest £240 at an interest rate of 5% p.a.

Make two columns, headed 'number of years' and 'amount'.
Follow the instructions in this flow chart, and write the result of carrying out each instruction in the proper column.

The entries in the columns start like this.

Number of years	Amount
0	£240
1	£252

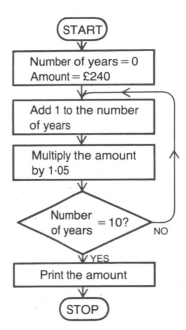

B10 Suppose you invest £40 and the rate of interest is 9% p.a.

The flow chart below is for answering the question 'How many years do I have to leave the money in for the amount to reach £100 or more?'

Make two columns as before, and follow the instructions.

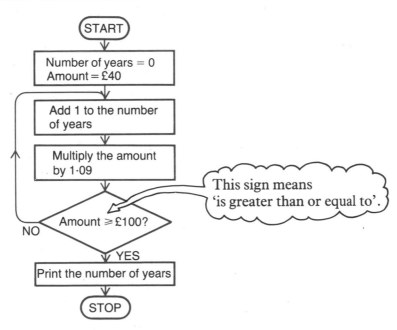

This sign means 'is greater than or equal to'.

B11 A car is worth £4500 when it is first bought, but its value drops by 15% each year. Draw **two** flow charts, for calculating
(a) the value of the car after 7 years
(b) the time taken for the value to drop below £500
Follow the instructions in your flow charts and give both answers.

12 Investigations (2)

A The Morse code

Samuel Morse invented a famous code in which the alphabet is represented by dots and dashes.

A · —	H · · · ·	O — — —	V · · · —
B — · · ·	I · ·	P · — — ·	W · — —
C — · — ·	J · — — —	Q — — · —	X — · · —
D — · ·	K — · —	R · — ·	Y — · — —
E ·	L · — · ·	S · · ·	Z — — · ·
F · · — ·	M — —	T —	
G — — ·	N — ·	U · · —	

A1   — · ·   — — — —

— ·   — — —   —

— · ·   ·   — · — ·   — — —   — · ·   ·

—   · · · ·   · ·   · · ·

— —   ·   · · ·   · · ·   · —   — — ·   ·

A2 Make up a Morse code for the Russian alphabet.

А	З	О	Х	Э
Б	И	П	Ц	Ю
В	Й	Р	Ч	Я
Г	К	С	Ш	
Д	Л	Т	Щ	
Е	М	У	Ы	
Ж	Н	Ф	Ь	

A3 When Morse designed his code, he gave the shortest possible sequences · and — to E and T. Suggest why he did this.

A4 We can classify sequences by the number of symbols in them.
For example, — · — — has 4 symbols.
If you are only allowed to use sequences with 1 symbol, then you can code only 2 letters. One will be · and the other —.
(a) How many **more** letters can you code if you can use sequences of 2 symbols as well?
(b) How many more can you code if you can use sequences of 3 symbols?
(c) How many more can you code if you can use sequences of 4 symbols?

A5 Explain why the number of extra letters you can code doubles each time you include sequences with one more symbol.

B How many sequences?

B1 (a) How many sequences are there with 1 dot and 0 dashes?
(b) How many with 1 dot and 1 dash?
(c) How many with 1 dot and 2 dashes?
(d) How many with 1 dot and 3 dashes?
(e) How many with 1 dot and 4 dashes?

B2 Make a table to show how many sequences there are with
1 dot and 0, 1, 2, 3, . . . dashes.

Number of dashes	0	1	2	3	4	5	6	7
Number of different sequences with 1 dot								

B3 You have taken account of every sequence with only 1 dot in it.
Now go on to sequences with 2 dots and various numbers of dashes.

How many different sequences are there with 2 dots and
(a) 0 dashes (b) 1 dash (c) 2 dashes (d) 3 dashes

B4 Before you go on to sequences with
3 dots, prepare this **two-way table**
to show the number of different
sequences in each case.

You can fill in the 1st and 2nd
rows of the table from your answers
so far.

Get as far as you can along the 3rd
row.

Number of dots	Number of dashes					
	0	1	2	3	4	5
1						
2						
3						
4						
5						

What patterns can you see in the numbers in the table?

Following the patterns, see if you can continue the table to find the
number of sequences with 4 dots and 4 dashes.

B5 The table you have made does not include sequences with 0 dots. So add another row at the top, so that it looks like this.

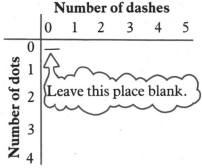

Number of dashes

(a) Think of sequences with 3 symbols altogether. They could have 2 dots and 1 dash, or 0 dot and 3 dashes, etc.
You can use the table to find out how many sequences there are with 3 symbols. Show how to do this.

(b) Show how you can find from the table how many sequences there are with 5 symbols.

B6 You are told that there are 817 190 different sequences with 14 dots and 9 dashes, and 490 314 different sequences with 15 dots and 8 dashes.

How many different sequences are there with 15 dots and 9 dashes? Can you explain why? (**Hint.** Every sequence must start with a dot or a dash.)

C 'Length' of a sequence

C1 Count a dot as 1 and a dash as 2.
So the 'length' of the sequence $\cdot - \cdot \cdot -$ is $1+2+1+1+2=7$.

Investigate how many sequences there are of length 1, 2, 3, . . .

Describe the pattern of the numbers you get.

Try to explain why you get that pattern.

C2 Do the same as before but with a dot counting as 1 and a dash counting as 3.

Algebra review (3)

1 (a) A car travelled for 120 miles at a speed of 40 m.p.h.
   How long did the journey take?

   (b) A car travelled for a miles at a speed of u m.p.h.
   Write an expression for the time taken, in hours.

   (c) A car did a return trip, a miles there and a miles back.
   On the way there it travelled at u m.p.h., and on the way
   back at v m.p.h. Write an expression for the total time
   taken, in hours.

   (d) A car did the same return trip, but this time taking x hours
   for the outward journey and y hours for the return journey.
   Write an expression for the average speed

      (i) for the outward journey

      (ii) for the return journey

      (iii) for the whole trip

2 (a) Write expressions for the angles
   marked a and b, in terms of x.

   (b) Use the fact that the angles of a
   triangle add up to 180° to write down
   an equation for x, and solve it
   to find x.

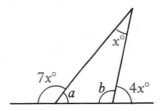

3 Multiply out the brackets in these expressions.

   (a) $(x + 3)^2$ (b) $(x - 4)^2$ (c) $(2x + 1)^2$

   (d) $(3x - 2)^2$ (e) $(5x + 4)^2$ (f) $(2 - 3x)^2$

4 (a) Here is a rule.

   To work out $(2\frac{1}{2})^2$, do $(2 \times 3) + \frac{1}{4}$
   To work out $(5\frac{1}{2})^2$, do $(5 \times 6) + \frac{1}{4}$
   To work out $(7\frac{1}{2})^2$, do $(7 \times 8) + \frac{1}{4}$, etc.

   Check that this rule works for the examples given.

   (b) Copy and complete this general statement of the rule:

   · To work out $(n + \frac{1}{2})^2$, do . . .

   (c) Multiply out the brackets in the expression $(n + \frac{1}{2})^2$ and
   explain **why** the rule works.

13 Right-angled triangles

A Pythagoras' rule

This diagram shows a right-angled triangle, with squares drawn on each of its sides.

The largest of the squares is the square on the **hypotenuse** (longest side) of the right-angled triangle.

Pythagoras' rule says that if you add together the areas of the two smaller squares, the result is equal to the area of the largest square.

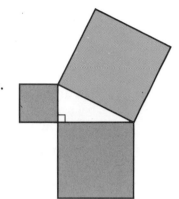

Another way to state Pythagoras' rule is this:

> The square on the hypotenuse is equal to the sum of the squares on the other two sides.

Pythagoras' rule can be used to calculate the length of one side of a right-angled triangle when the other two sides are known.

Calculating the hypotenuse

Suppose the two shorter sides of a right-angled triangle are 3 cm and 5 cm. You can calculate the hypotenuse like this.

1 Imagine the squares on the three sides. The areas of the two smaller ones are $9\,\text{cm}^2$ and $25\,\text{cm}^2$.

9 cm² 3 cm ? 5 cm 25 cm²

2 So the area of the largest square is $9 + 25 = 34\,\text{cm}^2$.

So the length of one side of it is $\sqrt{34}\,\text{cm} = \mathbf{5\cdot83}\,\text{cm}$ (to 2 d.p.).

34 cm² 5·83 cm

A1 Calculate the hypotenuse of a right-angled triangle whose other two sides are   (a) 4 cm and 5 cm (b) 9 cm and 12 cm (c) 7 cm and 7 cm (d) 6 cm and 16 cm

A2 The sides of a rectangle are 8 cm and 12 cm.
Calculate the length of one of its diagonals.

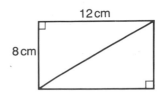

A3 Calculate the length of a diagonal of a square whose
sides are each 10 cm.

Calculating one of the shorter sides

Suppose the hypotenuse of a right-angled triangle is 7 cm and
one of the shorter sides is 4 cm. You can calculate the other side
like this.

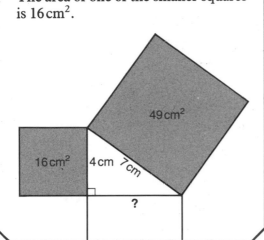

1 The area of the largest square is 49 cm². The area of one of the smaller squares is 16 cm².

49 cm²

16 cm² 4 cm 7 cm ?

2 So the area of the other square is 49 − 16 = 33 cm².

So the length of one side of it is $\sqrt{33}$ cm = **5·74 cm** (to 2 d.p.).

5·74 cm

33 cm²

A4 Calculate the length of the side marked **?** in each of
these right-angled triangles.

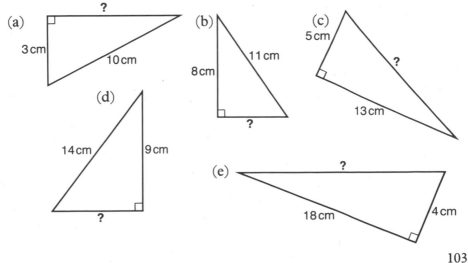

(a) ? 3 cm 10 cm

(b) 11 cm 8 cm ?

(c) 5 cm ? 13 cm

(d) 14 cm 9 cm ?

(e) ? 18 cm 4 cm

Let a, b and c stand for the lengths of the sides of a right-angled triangle, c being the hypotenuse.

The area of the square on side a is a^2.
The area of the square on side b is b^2.
The area of the square on side c is c^2.

So Pythagoras' rule can be written as a formula:

$$c^2 = a^2 + b^2.$$

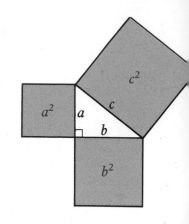

Using the formula: worked example

Suppose a is 8, c is 15 and we want to find b.

We substitute the known values into the formula $\quad c^2 = a^2 + b^2$.

$$\text{So} \quad 15^2 = 8^2 + b^2$$
$$\text{So} \quad 225 = 64 + b^2$$

Subtract 64 from both sides. $\quad 161 = b^2$

$$\text{So} \quad b = \sqrt{161} = \mathbf{12 \cdot 69} \quad \text{(to 2 d.p.)}$$

A5 Use the formula $c^2 = a^2 + b^2$ to calculate

(a) c when a is 4 and b is 6   (b) a when b is 2 and c is 5

(c) b when a is 7 and c is 8   (d) a when b is 3·2 and c is 12·7

A6 An equilateral triangle can be split into two identical (congruent) right-angled triangles, as shown here.

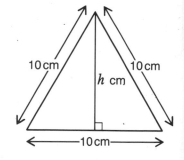

(a) Use Pythagoras' rule to calculate the height h cm of an equilateral triangle whose sides are each 10 cm long.

(b) Calculate the area of the equilateral triangle.

A7 Sketch an isosceles triangle ABC whose base BC is 6 cm and whose other two sides AB and AC are each 9 cm.

(a) Use Pythagoras' rule to calculate the height of the isosceles triangle.

(b) Calculate the area of the triangle.

A8 The four sides of a rhombus are each 8 cm, and one diagonal is 5 cm. Calculate the length of the other diagonal.

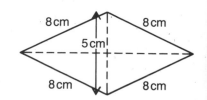

A9 Two vertical posts are 4 m apart on horizontal ground. One is 5 m tall and the other 7 m tall.

Draw a sketch, and calculate the distance between the tops of the posts. (**Hint.** Add to your sketch the horizontal line through the top of the shorter post.)

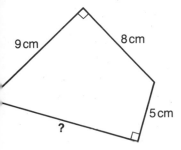

A10 Calculate the length of the fourth side of the quadrilateral on the left.

A11 Calculate the distance between opposite corners of a cube whose edges are 5 cm long.

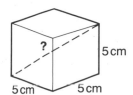

B The distance between two points whose coordinates are given

A is the point $(1, {}^-2)$ and B is $(4, 3)$.

The distance between A and B is the length AB. This length is the hypotenuse of a right-angled triangle whose other sides are 3 units and 5 units.

So $AB^2 = 3^2 + 5^2 = 9 + 25 = 34$.

AB^2 means the square of the length AB. AB is treated like a single letter; it does not mean $A \times B$ here.

So AB must be $\sqrt{34}$ or $5 \cdot 83$ (to 2 d.p.).

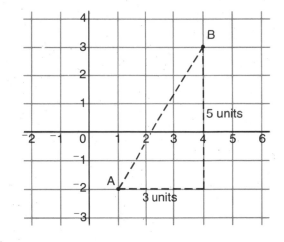

B1 Sketch a grid and mark the points P $({}^-2, 1)$ and Q $(5, 3)$. Calculate the distance from P to Q, to 2 d.p.

B2 Calculate to 2 d.p. the distance between $(1, 0)$ and $(6, {}^-2)$.

B3 Calculate the distance between each of these pairs of points.
(a) $(0, 2)$ and $(6, 0)$ (b) $(0, 2)$ and $(4, {}^-1)$
(c) $({}^-2, {}^-3)$ and $(5, {}^-1)$ (d) $(4, 3)$ and $({}^-2, {}^-4)$

B4 A circle is drawn with its centre at $(0, 0)$ and radius 20 units. Without drawing, work out whether these points are inside the circle, on the circle or outside the circle.

(a) $(5, 19)$ (b) $(10, 18)$ (c) $(12, 16)$ (d) $(18, 7)$ (e) $({}^-6, 19)$

B5 A is the point $(1, 2)$, B is $(7, 4)$ and C is $(4, 8)$.
Calculate the length of each side of the triangle ABC.

B6 Find by calculation which two of these points are closest
together, and which two are furthest apart.

A $(20, 18)$ B $(27, 40)$ C $(42, 40)$ D $(35, 15)$

B7 To get from a point O to a point P you go 4 km east and 5 km north.
To get from O to Q you go 3 km west and 6 km south.

Calculate the distance between P and Q.

C Proving Pythagoras' rule

Pythagoras' rule says that in **any** right-angled
triangle, the area of the square on the hypotenuse
is equal to the sum of the areas of the squares
on the other two sides.

In the diagram on the right the red area, c^2, is
equal to the grey area, $a^2 + b^2$, no matter what
a and b are, as long as the white triangle is
right-angled.

How can we be sure that the rule is always
true? Or in other words, how can we **prove** that
the red area must be equal to the grey area?

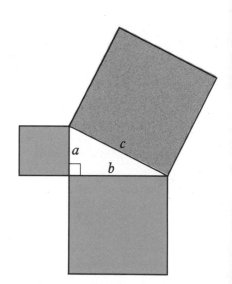

C1 Look at the two diagrams below. They show two different ways
of splitting up a square whose sides are $(a + b)$.

From these diagrams you can show that the red area **must** be
the same as the grey area. In other words you can prove that
Pythagoras' rule is true. Can you see how? Write down your explanation.

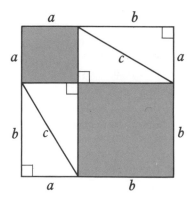

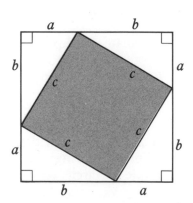

D Acute angles and obtuse angles in triangles

An **acute** angle is one which is less than 90°.
An **obtuse** angle is one which is greater than 90°
but less than 180°.

Acute angle   Obtuse angle

Suppose the two 'arms' of an angle are 7 cm long and 5 cm long.
In these diagrams the arms are OP and OQ.

As the angle at O gets larger, ... the distance PQ gets larger.

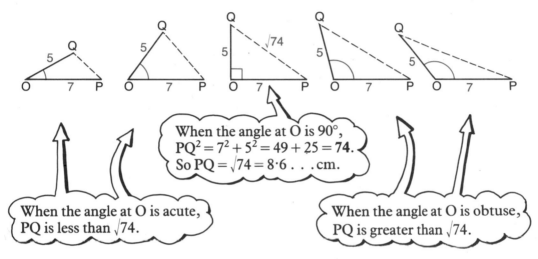

When the angle at O is 90°,
$PQ^2 = 7^2 + 5^2 = 49 + 25 = \textbf{74}$.
So $PQ = \sqrt{74} = 8\cdot6 \ldots$ cm.

When the angle at O is acute,
PQ is less than $\sqrt{74}$.

When the angle at O is obtuse,
PQ is greater than $\sqrt{74}$.

When you are given the lengths of the sides of a triangle (**any** triangle),
you can use Pythagoras' rule to decide whether each angle is acute,
obtuse, or a right-angle.

Worked example

In the triangle ABC, AB = 4 cm, BC = 6 cm and AC = 7 cm.
Is the angle at B acute, obtuse or a right-angle?

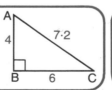

If the angle at B were a
right-angle, then AC^2 would
be $4^2 + 6^2 = 16 + 36 = 52$.
So AC would be $\sqrt{52} = 7\cdot2 \ldots$

But we are told that
AC is only 7 cm. So
the angle at B must
be **acute**.

> **D1** In the triangle PQR, PQ = 7 cm, QR = 9 cm and PR = 12 cm.
> (a) Is the angle at Q acute, obtuse, or a right-angle?
> (b) What about the angles at P and at R?
>
> **D2** Find out whether each angle of the triangle XYZ is acute,
> obtuse, or a right-angle when
> (a) XY = 8 cm, YZ = 12 cm, XZ = 9 cm
> (b) XY = 12 cm, YZ = 5 cm, XZ = 11 cm

E A nomogram for Pythagoras' rule

A nomogram consists of a set of scales which can be used to calculate numbers which are related by a formula.

The formula in this case is

$$c^2 = a^2 + b^2.$$

Suppose a is 6·5 and b is 7·3 and you want to know c.

Put a ruler across the nomogram so that it crosses the a-scale at 6·5 and the b-scale at 7·3.

You can read off the value of c where the ruler crosses the c-scale.

The nomogram can be used in a similar way to find a when b and c are known, or b when a and c are known.

Nomograms are used by people who need to use the same formula again and again. The answers given by a nomogram are only rough, but they may be good enough.

E1 Use the nomogram to find

    (a) c when $a = 6·1$, $b = 7·6$

    (b) a when $b = 5·5$, $c = 9·1$

    (c) b when $a = 4·8$, $c = 10·3$

E2 In the triangle XYZ, XY = 4cm, YZ = 7cm and XZ = 9cm.

Use the nomogram to find out if the angle at Y is acute, obtuse or a right-angle. Explain how you do it.

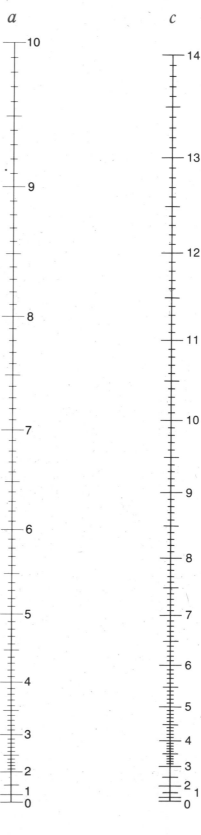

F Three-dimensional problems

A cube has two kinds of diagonal.

A **face diagonal** is a line joining
opposite vertices of one face.

A **body diagonal** is a line joining
opposite vertices of the cube.

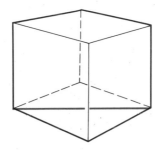

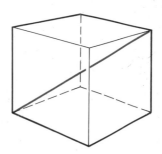

Suppose each edge of the cube is 10 cm long.

Then a face diagonal f cm is the
hypotenuse of a right-angled
triangle whose other sides are
both 10 cm.

And a body diagonal b cm is the
hypotenuse of a right-angled triangle
whose other sides are 10 cm and f cm.

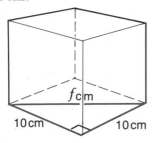

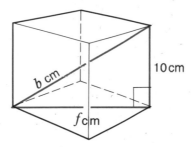

F1 (a) Calculate the length of a face diagonal of a cube
whose edges are 10 cm long.

(b) Calculate the length of a body diagonal of the cube.

To calculate the body diagonal, it was first necessary to calculate
the face diagonal. If you are trying to calculate a length in three
dimensions, it is often necessary to calculate another length first.
Also, you have to find right-angled triangles. Sometimes you need to
add extra lines to see them.

F2 Calculate the length d cm of the
(body) diagonal of this cuboid.

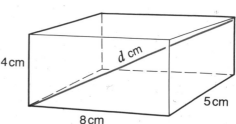

F3   Sketch a cuboid 3 cm by 4 cm by 5 cm.
Calculate the length of its diagonal.

(By itself, 'diagonal' means 'body diagonal'.)

Right-angles in three dimensions

A vertical line and a horizontal plane give the clearest
example of a line at right-angles to a plane.

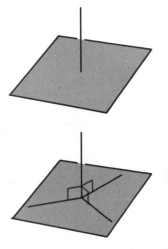

When a line is at right-angles to a plane, it is at
right-angles to **every** line which lies in the plane.

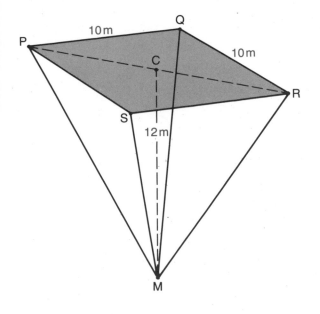

F4   P, Q, R and S are four points on
the horizontal ceiling of a concert
hall. PQRS is a square whose
sides are each of length 10 m.

C is the centre of the square.

A microphone M is attached to P, Q,
R and S by four wires of equal length.
The microphone has to hang directly
below C, and the distance CM has to
be 12 m.

(a)   Triangle PQR is a right-angled
triangle. Which of its angles is a
right-angle?

(b)   Calculate the distance PR, and
hence PC.

(c)   Triangle PCM is a right-angled
triangle. Which of its angles is a
right-angle?

(d)   Calculate the length of the wire PM

F5   If the four wires in the diagram above are replaced by
wires of length 9 m each, how far below the ceiling will the
microphone hang?

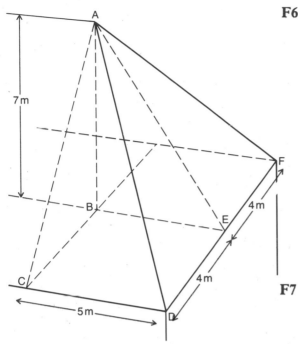

F6 This diagram shows part of the roof of a building.

The point A is directly above the point B. BCDE is a horizontal rectangle.

(a) Calculate the length AC.

(b) Calculate the length of the sloping edge AD.

(c) Calculate the length AE.

(d) Calculate the area of the sloping face ADF.

F7 The diagrams below show a square-based pyramid whose base is 8 cm by 8 cm and whose height is 6 cm.

Each diagram shows a different way of calculating the length of a slanting edge of the pyramid.

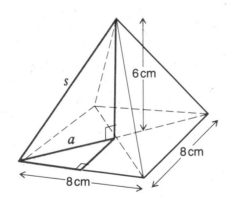 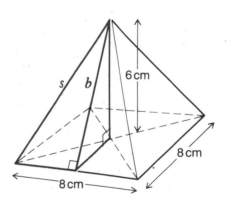

(a) Calculate the length *s* by first calculating the length *a*.

(b) Calculate *s* by first calculating *b*.

(c) Calculate the area of one of the sloping faces.

F8 Sketch a square-based pyramid whose base is 10 cm square and whose height is 5 cm.

Calculate the length of a slanting edge of the pyramid.

G Trigonometry

Pythagoras' rule connects the lengths of the sides of a right-angled triangle. Trigonometry connects the sides and angles.

As a reminder, here are the three basic formulas of trigonometry.

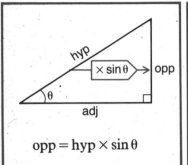

$$\text{opp} = \text{hyp} \times \sin \theta$$

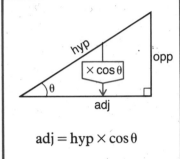

$$\text{adj} = \text{hyp} \times \cos \theta$$

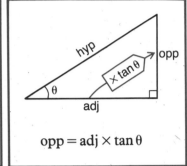

$$\text{opp} = \text{adj} \times \tan \theta$$

Worked example (1): calculating a side

Calculate the side marked a in this right-angled triangle.

The sides are labelled 'hyp, opp, adj' in relation to the given angle of 35°.

'Opp' is known and 'hyp' is wanted. So the **sine** must be used.

$$\text{opp} = \text{hyp} \times \sin \theta$$
$$7 = a \times \sin 35°$$
$$\frac{7}{\sin 35°} = a$$

On a calculator, $\dfrac{7}{\sin 35°} = 12{\cdot}204. \ . \ .$ So $a = \mathbf{12{\cdot}2}$ (to 1 d.p.).

(Key sequence, on most calculators: $\boxed{7}\ \boxed{\div}\ \boxed{3}\ \boxed{5}\ \boxed{\sin}\ \boxed{=}$)

Worked example (2): calculating an angle

Calculate the angle marked b in this right-angled triangle.

The sides are labelled 'hyp', etc. in relation to the angle b. 'Hyp' and 'adj' are known. So the **cosine** must be used.

$$\text{adj} = \text{hyp} \times \cos b$$
$$4 = 9 \times \cos b$$
$$\frac{4}{9} = \cos b$$

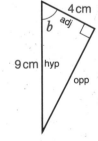

So b is the **inverse cosine** of $\dfrac{4}{9}$. On a calculator, $b = \mathbf{63{\cdot}6°}$ (to 1 d.p.).

(Key sequence, on most calculators: $\boxed{4}\ \boxed{\div}\ \boxed{9}\ \boxed{=}\ \boxed{\text{inv}}\ \boxed{\cos}$)

G1   Calculate the sides and angles marked with letters, to 1 d.p.

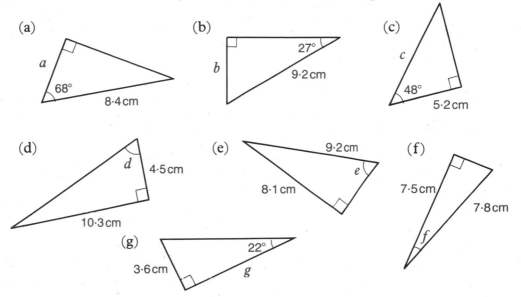

(a)

a

68°

8·4 cm

(b)

27°

b

9·2 cm

(c)

c

48°

5·2 cm

(d)

d 4·5 cm

10·3 cm

(e)

9·2 cm

e

8·1 cm

(f)

7·5 cm

7·8 cm

f

(g)

3·6 cm

22°

g

G2   Calculate the sides marked with letters.

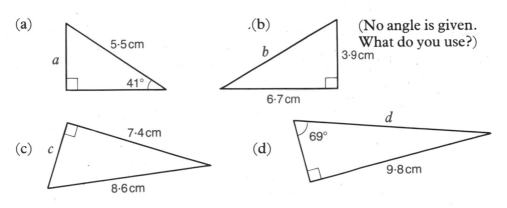

(a)

5·5 cm

a

41°

(b)

b

3·9 cm

6·7 cm

(No angle is given.
What do you use?)

(c) c

7·4 cm

8·6 cm

(d)

69°

d

9·8 cm

The 'height' of a triangle does not mean anything
unless you have first chosen one side as the **base**.
Then the height is measured at right-angles to
the base.

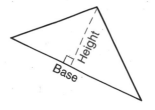

Height

Base

G3   The line showing the height of triangle ABC
splits the triangle into two right-angled triangles.

(a)   Use one of the right-angled triangles to
calculate the height of triangle ABC.

(b)   Calculate the area of triangle ABC.

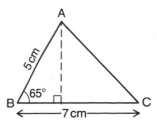

A

5 cm

65°

B

7 cm

C

G4 Copy this sketch of a triangle PQR.
(Do not make an accurate drawing.)

Take PR as the base. Draw a line
to show the height of the triangle.
(a) Calculate the height.
(b) Calculate the area.

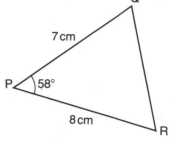

G5 Sketch the same triangle PQR again.
This time, take PQ as the base. Draw a line to show the height.

(a) Calculate the height.
(b) Calculate the area.
(c) Could you calculate the area using QR as base,
given only the measurements in the diagram?

G6 Sketch a triangle ABC in which angle A is 40°, AB is 6 cm,
and AC is 10 cm. Calculate the area of the triangle.

G7

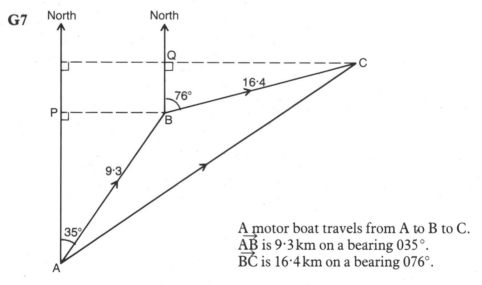

A motor boat travels from A to B to C.
$\vec{AB}$ is 9·3 km on a bearing 035°.
$\vec{BC}$ is 16·4 km on a bearing 076°.

(a) Calculate how far B is north of A (the distance AP in the diagram).
(b) Calculate how far B is east of A (the distance PB).
(c) Calculate how far C is north of B (the distance BQ).
(d) Calculate how far C is east of B (the distance QC).
(e) How far is C (i) north (ii) east of A?
(f) Calculate the distance between A and C.
(g) Calculate the bearing of $\vec{AC}$.

G8 Re-do question G7 when $\vec{AB}$ is 10·2 km on a bearing 069° and
BC is 6·6 km on a bearing 018°.

G9 Re-do question G7 when $\vec{AB}$ is 20 km on a bearing 040° and
BC is 10 km on a bearing 110°. (In part (c), for 'north' read 'south'.)

114

Review 2

8 Direct and inverse proportionality

8.1 In an electroplating process, the amount of copper deposited in one hour is proportional to the strength of the current.

When the current is 15·5 amps, the mass deposited is 36·7 g.

(a) Calculate the mass deposited when the current is 10 amps.
(b) Calculate the strength of the current needed to deposit 50 g of copper in one hour.

8.2 The density of a sample of a gas is inversely proportional to its volume. When the volume is $2 \cdot 4 \, \text{m}^3$, the density is $1 \cdot 4 \, \text{kg/m}^3$. Calculate

(a) the density when the volume is $1 \cdot 5 \, \text{m}^3$
(b) the volume when the density is $0 \cdot 4 \, \text{kg/m}^3$

8.3 A banjo string 38 cm long is tuned to the note B whose frequency is 496 Hz.

What length of the string will give the note D whose frequency is 588 Hz?

9 Representing information

9.1 Mary, Jeff, Hitesh, Karen, Gary and Sadia are six pupils in a school. The following pairs are friends:
Mary and Sadia, Jeff and Hitesh, Jeff and Karen, Jeff and Gary, Karen and Hitesh, Karen and Sadia.

(a) Can they sit down in a row of six seats so that people sitting next to one another are friends? How many different ways are there to seat them?

(b) Can they sit in a circle so that each person has a friend on either side?

Jeff falls out with Hitesh, so they don't want to sit next to each other. Mary and Gary fall in love.

(c) Is it now possible for the six people to sit in a row? In how many ways can they be seated?

(d) Is it now possible for them to sit in a circle?

(e) Could they sit in a circle if Hitesh and Sadia became friends? In how many ways can they be seated?

9.2 64% of the population of Ruritania have blue eyes and 23% have fair hair. 19% have neither blue eyes nor fair hair.

What percentage of the population have blue eyes and fair hair?

9.3 (a) What information about the network is contained in the first row of the table?

(b) Copy and complete the table.

(c) Why is the sum of the numbers in every column equal to 2?

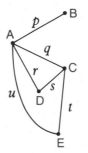

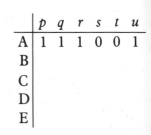

	p	q	r	s	t	u
A	1	1	1	0	0	1
B						
C						
D						
E						

10 Looking at data

10.1 The weights, in kg, of the girls in a hockey team are

50   55   45   57   58   46   51   58   53   48   43

(a) What is the range of the weights?

(b) What is the median weight?

(c) The girl who weighs 55 kg is replaced in the team by a girl who weighs 45 kg.
What is the new median weight of the team?

10.2 These are the weights, in kg, of 25 boys and 30 girls all aged 15.

Boys   53   59   70   53   50   48   62   66   69   55

47   53   54   53   60   53   47   44   70   73

44   60   53   58   41

Girls   63   50   54   60   39   54   54   68   49   42

70   58   57   47   48   55   35   64   47   48

50   52   54   40   54   40   54   49   62   48

(a) Make a stem-and-leaf table for each set of data.

(b) Summarise each set of data by giving the smallest, median, largest and range.

11 Percentage (2)

11.1 A drying machine reduces the water content of carrots by 20% each time it is used. What percentage water reduction do you get overall, when you use the machine twice?

11.2 Traffic enters the road system at A. 35% of it turns left and 65% right.

45% of the traffic arriving at B turns left and 55% right.

20% of the traffic arriving at C turns left and 80% right.

What percentage of the traffic entering at A gets to (a) D (b) E (c) F

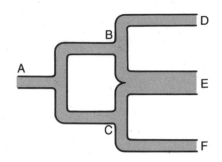

11.3 Calculate the overall percentage increase or decrease after

(a) a 21% increase followed by a 36% increase
(b) an 18% decrease followed by a 14% decrease
(c) an 8% increase followed by a 24% decrease

11.4 On 1st September 1986, Ms Skint borrows £800 from a bank. The bank charges interest on the loan at a rate of 2% per month.

By the last day of September, the amount owed by Ms Skint has gone up by 2%, so she then owes £800 × 1·02 = £816. On that day she pays the bank £100, so the amount she owes on 1st October is £716. (We say the **outstanding amount** on 1st October is £716.)

By the last day of October, the amount has gone up by 2% again to £716 × 1·02 = £730·32. Once again Ms Skint pays back £100, so the outstanding amount on 1st November is £630·32.

The same thing happens at the end of every month.

Make two columns headed 'Date' and 'Outstanding amount'.

Follow the instructions in this flow chart.

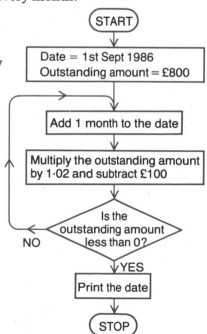

117

13 Right-angled triangles

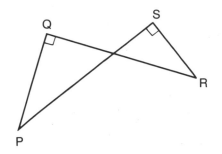

13.1 In this diagram, PQ = 4 cm,
QR = 7 cm and RS = 3 cm.

Calculate PS.

13.2 Calculate the distance between the points ($^-$2, 3) and (3, 9).

13.3 Think of AB as the base of this triangle.

(a) Calculate the height of the triangle.

(b) Calculate the area of the triangle.

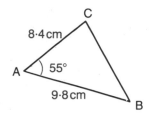

13.4 In the triangle ABC, AB = 8 cm, BC = 11 cm and AC = 17 cm.

(a) Sketch the triangle. Which angle is the largest?

(b) Find out by calculation whether this angle is equal to, greater than, or less than 90°.

13.5 Sketch a cuboid 5 cm by 5 cm by 10 cm.

Calculate the length of one of its body diagonals (a line from one corner to an opposite corner).

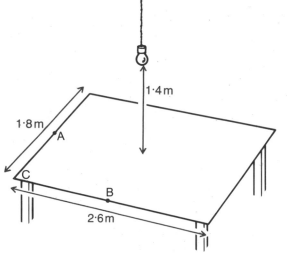

13.6 A lamp hangs directly above the centre of a rectangle table.

The table is 2·6 m by 1·8 m, and the lamp hangs 1·4 m above the table.

Calculate the distance of each of these points from the lamp.

(a) A, the midpoint of one of the shorter edges of the table

(b) B, the midpoint of one of the longer edges

(c) C, a corner of the table

14 Volume

A Cuboids and prisms

In this chapter we shall be looking at objects whose volumes can be calculated.

The simplest kind of object whose volume can be calculated is a rectangular block or **cuboid**.

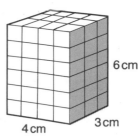

The cuboid shown on the right is made from 1 cm cubes.
It is made up of layers, each containing 3×4 cubes.
There are 6 layers, so the volume is $3 \times 4 \times 6\,\text{cm}^3$.

There is nothing special about the numbers 3, 4 and 6.
To find the volume of any cuboid you multiply length × width × height.

A1 Calculate, to the nearest $0.1\,\text{cm}^3$, the volume of a cuboid 4·6 cm by 3·8 cm by 9·4 cm.

A2 A rectangular swimming pool is 6·5 m long and 4·4 m wide. When it is full, the water is 1·5 m deep throughout.

Calculate the volume of the water (a) in m^3 (b) in litres ($1\,\text{m}^3 = 1000\,l$.)

A3 Estimate the volume of the room you are now in. Compare your estimate with those of other people.

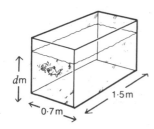

A4 A fish tank is 1·5 m long and 0·7 m wide. It contains $0.55\,\text{m}^3$ of water.

Let d m be the depth of the water.
Then $1.5 \times 0.7 \times d = 0.55$.

Calculate d to the nearest 0·1 m.

A5 A rectangular pond is 3·7 m by 2·6 m. The water in it is the same depth throughout. Calculate the depth if the volume of water is

(a) $4.8\,\text{m}^3$ (b) 750 litres

A6 The liquid in this closed container is 9 cm deep.

How deep will it be if the container is turned over so that it stands on one of its rectangular faces?

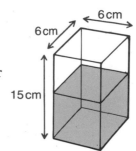

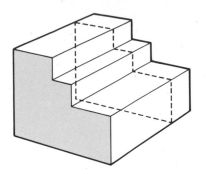

This object is an example of a **prism**.

Wherever you slice it parallel to the shaded end face you get a **cross-section** which is identical to the end face.

This prism can be thought of as made up of cuboids, each 1 cm by 1 cm by 7 cm.

The volume of each one of these cuboids is 7 cm^3.

There are 15 of these cuboids altogether, because the area of the cross-section is 15 cm^2.

So the total volume of the prism $= 15 \times 7$
$$= 105 \text{ cm}^3$$

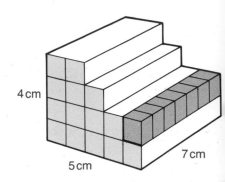

Volume of prism = area of cross-section × length

A7 Calculate the volume of each of these prisms. All measurements are in cm.

(a)

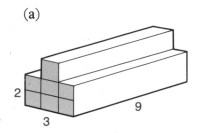

(b)

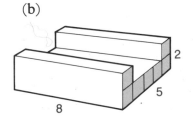

(c)

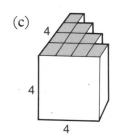

A8 (a) Estimate the area of the cross-section of this prism.

(b) Estimate the volume of the prism, which is 3·5 cm long.

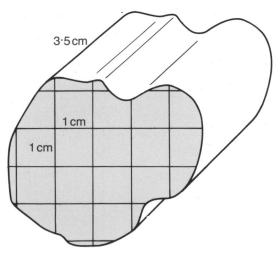

A9 (a) Calculate the cross-sectional area of this prism.

(b) Calculate the volume of the prism.

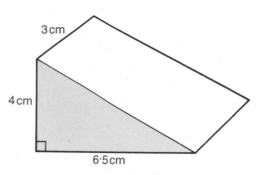

A10 Calculate (i) the cross-sectional area (ii) the volume of each of these prisms.

(a)

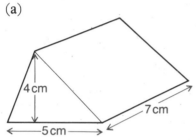

(b)

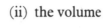

A shape cut out from card is a prism.
The 'cross-section' is the shape cut out.
The 'length' is the thickness of the card.

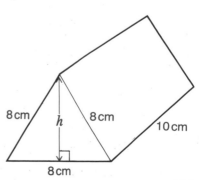

Volume = Area × Thickness

A11 A piece whose area is 45 cm² is cut from a sheet of metal 0·3 cm thick. Calculate the volume of the piece.

A12 A piece of plastic whose volume is 20·8 cm³ is cut from a sheet 0·4 cm thick. Calculate the area of the piece.

A13 On the side of a 1-litre tin of paint it says that the paint will cover 4·5 m² (45 000 cm²). Calculate the thickness of the coat of paint, to 1 s.f. (1 litre = 1000 cm³.)

A14 The cross-section of this prism is an equilateral triangle with sides 8 cm long.

(a) Calculate the height marked h.

(b) Calculate the cross-sectional area of the prism.

(c) Calculate the volume of the prism.

(d) How much does the prism weigh if it is made from glass of density 2·6 g/cm³?

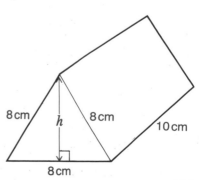

B Cylinders

A prism whose cross-section is a circle is called a **cylinder**.

If the radius of the cylinder is r, the cross-sectional area can be calculated by using the formula for the area of a circle (πr^2).

As with any other prism, volume = cross-sectional area × length.

B1 A cylinder's radius is 4·0 cm and its length is 7·5 cm.
Calculate   (a) its cross-sectional area   (b) its volume

B2 (a) Calculate the volume of this rolling pin.

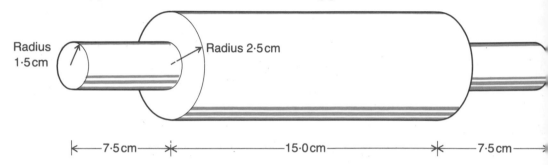

Radius 1·5 cm

Radius 2·5 cm

|←—7·5 cm—→|←————————15·0 cm————————→|←—7·5 cm—→|

(b) How much will the rolling pin weigh if it is made from wood whose density is 0·9 g/cm³?

B3 (a) Without using a calculator, estimate the volume in litres of the water in each container shown here.

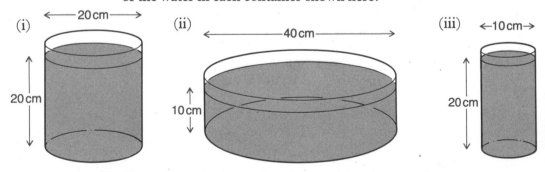

(i) ←—20 cm—→   20 cm

(ii) ←————40 cm————→   10 cm

(iii) ←10 cm→   20 cm

(b) Now use a calculator to work out each volume and see how good your estimates were.

B4 An oil drum is about 1 metre tall and its diameter is about 80 cm. Estimate its volume in litres without using a calculator.

B5 A and B are two cylinders. They are the same height, but the diameter of A is twice that of B. What can you say about the volumes of the two cylinders?

C Pyramids and cones

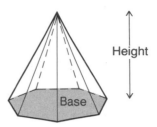

It can be shown that the volume of a pyramid is $\dfrac{\text{area of base} \times \text{height}}{3}$.

C1 Sketch a pyramid whose base is a square 4 cm by 4 cm and whose height is 5 cm. Calculate its volume.

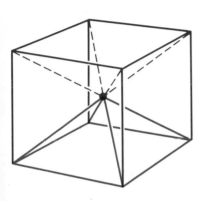

C2 If all the corners of a cube are joined to the centre, then six identical pyramids are formed. One of them is shown coloured in this diagram.

Suppose each edge of the cube is 6 cm long.

(a) Calculate the volume of one of the pyramids, starting from the fact that six of them make up the cube.

(b) Now calculate the volume of one of the pyramids using the formula for the volume of a pyramid.

A cone is a pyramid with a circular base. If the base radius is r and the height is h,

then the volume $= \dfrac{\text{area of base} \times \text{height}}{3}$

$= \dfrac{\pi r^2 h}{3}$

C3 Use the formula $V = \dfrac{\pi r^2 h}{3}$ to calculate V when $r = 5$ and $h = 12$.

C4 Re-arrange the formula $V = \dfrac{\pi r^2 h}{3}$ to make h the subject.

C5 If $V = \dfrac{\pi r^2 h}{3}$ and V is 200 and h is 10, calculate r to 1 d.p.

C6 (a) Would you say that this cone is about 60% full, 50% full, 40% full, 30% full, 20% full or 10% full?

(b) Use a calculator to work out what percentage of the volume of the cone is filled.

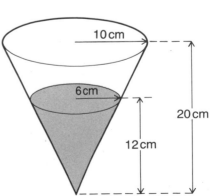

123

15 Problems in planning

A Holidays

In the office at Mayhem's stores, everybody gets a fortnight's holiday.
(People are not allowed to take two separate weeks.)

The store manager gets first choice.
If the store manager is away, her secretary must be present.
If the chief buyer is away, his secretary must be present.
The two secretaries cannot be away at the same time.

The chief cashier is married to the transport supervisor, so they
always take their holidays together.

There must be at least four people present at any time.

In the office there is a chart for planning holidays.

There are six pieces of grey card which can be moved around.

Each piece represents someone's holiday.

Summer Holiday Planner

Week no.	1	2	3	4	5	6	7	8
Store manager		▓	▓					
Store manager's secretary				▓				
Chief cashier	▓	▓						
Chief buyer						▓	▓	
Chief buyer's secretary					▓	▓		
Transport supervisor	▓	▓						

A1 There are three things wrong with the holiday plan shown.
What are they?

A2 Copy the planner on squared paper, without the grey pieces.
Cut out the six pieces from paper or card.
Try to make a holiday plan by moving the pieces around, but
keep the store manager's holiday in weeks 2 and 3.

When you think you have a plan which does not break any of
the rules, ask someone to check it. Then shade where the pieces go.

A3 (a) Is it possible to squeeze all the holidays into only 7 weeks
instead of 8? Does the store manager have to change her weeks?

(b) Is it possible to squeeze them all into 6 weeks?

A4 The full-time staff of a sports centre are
the manager, the caretaker, two clerical staff, two instructors.

Make an 8-week holiday plan for them, following these rules:

Everybody gets a fortnight's holiday (two weeks together), except the caretaker; he gets 3 weeks off and insists on having weeks 2, 3 and 4.

There must not be more than two people off at any one time.

The clerical staff cannot be off together.

The instructors cannot be off together.

If the caretaker is off, there must be two instructors present.

A5 Can the holidays in question A4 be squeezed into 7 weeks?

B Work

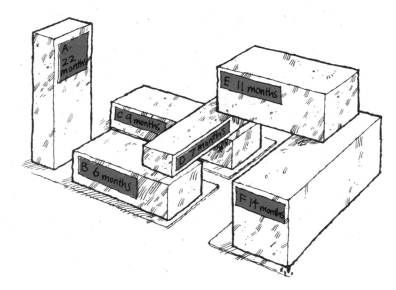

B1 This picture shows an architect's model for a new office complex. The labels show how long each block will take to build.

Each block is to be built by a different firm of builders, so two or more blocks can be worked on at the same time.

Obviously the blocks cannot be built in any order. For example, block D cannot be started until blocks B and C are both finished.

(a) If the builder of block D wanted to start work on 1st November, what would be the latest date for starting to build (i) block B (ii) block C

(b) The City Council decides that the whole complex must be finished by 1st January 1994.
   (i) What is the latest possible date for starting work on each of the blocks?
   (ii) Which block needs to be started first?
   (iii) How long does it take between starting work on the first block and finishing the complex?

125

Here is a list of the jobs involved in making a woman's suit, together with
an estimate of the time it takes one person to do each job.

Pin pattern to fabric and cut out pieces	1 hour
Mark darts on jacket pieces	$\frac{3}{4}$ hour
Tack together jacket pieces	1 hour
Fit and adjust jacket	$\frac{1}{4}$ hour
Stitch jacket together	$1\frac{1}{4}$ hour
Adjust sleeve length and sew on cuffs	$\frac{1}{2}$ hour
Mark darts on skirt pieces	$\frac{1}{4}$ hour
Tack together skirt pieces	$\frac{1}{2}$ hour
Fit and adjust skirt pieces	$\frac{1}{4}$ hour
Stitch skirt together	$\frac{1}{4}$ hour
Tack and stitch waistband together	$\frac{1}{2}$ hour
Fit waistband to skirt	$\frac{1}{4}$ hour
Tack and sew zip on to skirt	$\frac{1}{2}$ hour
Adjust and sew skirt hem	$\frac{1}{4}$ hour

B2 Add up the times for the jobs.
Your answer gives an estimate of the time the work would take
if there was only one person working on it.

If the customer wanted the suit in a hurry – say 5 hours – could this be
done by using more people? The answer is not obvious, because many jobs
cannot be shared out, and certain jobs cannot be started until others
are finished. For example, you cannot fix the waistband on to the skirt if
the skirt has not been sewn together yet.

Here is a diagram showing how the jobs can be shared out between
three people. The jobs done by each person have to be done in order, from
left to right. The arrows show where starting a job depends on some other
job being finished. For instance, the second person cannot mark darts on the
skirt pieces until the first person has cut them out.

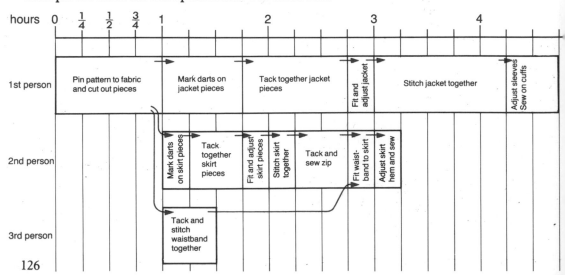

126

B3 (a) With three people working as shown, how long will it take to finish the suit?

(b) What effect will there be on the overall time taken to finish the work if the first person takes $\frac{1}{4}$ hour longer to tack together the jacket pieces?

(c) What effect will there be on the overall time if the second person takes $\frac{1}{4}$ hour longer to tack and sew the zip?

(d) What effect will there be on the overall time if the third person takes 1 hour longer to tack and stitch the waistband together?

B4 If everybody takes the estimated time originally given for each job, could the second person start later than shown in the diagram? How much later?

B5 If the second person starts as late as possible, how late could the third person start work on the waistband?

Jan, Rob and Cathy are decorating their flat. This table shows the various stages of the work. 'Time needed' includes time for the paint to dry.

Job	Time needed	What needs to be finished before this job is started
Sand and prime woodwork	1 day	
Undercoat on woodwork	1 day	Woodwork primed
First coat on woodwork	1 day	Undercoat on woodwork
Top coat on woodwork	1 day	First coat on woodwork
Strip off wallpaper	1 day	
Repair wall plaster	1 day	Wallpaper stripped off
Paper walls	2 days	Top coat on woodwork, wall plaster repaired, second coat on ceilings
Repair ceilings	1 day	
First coat on ceilings	1 day	Ceilings repaired
Second coat on ceilings	1 day	First coat on ceilings

B6 Jan agrees to start by sanding and priming the woodwork.
Rob says he will start by stripping off the old wallpaper.
Which job must Cathy start on?

B7 Make a plan of work for the three people.

This is how Jan's work starts.

days 0   1   2

Jan | Sand and prime woodwork | Undercoat on woodwork |

c Other planning problems

C1 To get a Ruritanian passport takes 4 weeks from the time of applying. You need an identity card to apply, and getting an identity card takes 5 weeks. When you send for the identity card you should remember to enclose a duplicate birth certificate (it takes 4 weeks to get one of these) and a certified photograph of yourself (one of these takes 2 weeks).

An alternative is to start by getting a certificate of official search. This takes 6 weeks. Send it off with a certified photograph and a duplicate birth certificate. In 3 weeks you will get a priority voucher. A priority voucher will enable you to apply for a passport without having an identity card. Passports obtained by priority voucher take 5 weeks, but this can be reduced to 3 weeks by payment of an expediting premium.

(a) What is the quickest way to get a Ruritanian passport?

(b) How long does it take?

C2 When school parties visit the Cold Comfort farm museum, they can go on the 'complete tour' or the 'mini-tour'.

The complete tour lasts $2\frac{1}{2}$ hours; the mini-tour lasts $1\frac{1}{2}$ hours.

The curator of the museum has to arrange the times when the school parties go on tour. This is a list of the schools that have requested tours on Monday.

Name of school	Number of pupils	Length of tour
Reydon	17	$1\frac{1}{2}$ hours
Chalkstone	23	$2\frac{1}{2}$ hours
St Louis	12	$1\frac{1}{2}$ hours
Westbourne	32	$2\frac{1}{2}$ hours
Orwell	25	$1\frac{1}{2}$ hours
Uplands	38	$1\frac{1}{2}$ hours
Blackbourne	19	$1\frac{1}{2}$ hours

The farm museum opens from 10:00 a.m. to 6:00 p.m., but tours are not possible between 1:00 p.m. and 2:00 p.m. because the tour guides have their lunch then. To prevent congestion, no more than 50 pupils may be going round the museum at one moment.

Try to fit all the schools in. Draw a diagram if it helps you.

16 Linear equations

A Some puzzles

A1 3 bulbs and 4 batteries cost 69p.
1 bulb and 2 batteries cost 31p.

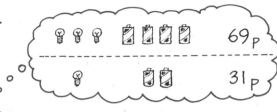

What do the following cost?

(a) 6 bulbs and 8 batteries

(b) 4 bulbs and 6 batteries

(c) 2 bulbs and 2 batteries

(d) 1 bulb and 1 battery

(e) 1 battery
(Remember that 1 bulb and
2 batteries cost 31p.)

(f) 1 bulb

A2   4 nuts and 2 bolts weigh 17 grams.
3 nuts and 5 bolts weigh 32 grams.

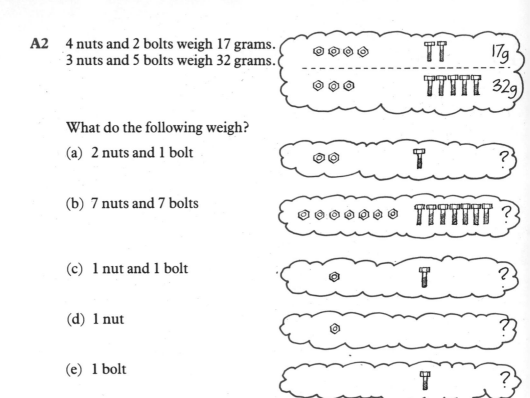

What do the following weigh?

(a) 2 nuts and 1 bolt

(b) 7 nuts and 7 bolts

(c) 1 nut and 1 bolt

(d) 1 nut

(e) 1 bolt

A3   Kate's dad is a milkman, and is working out his weekly bills.
Each customer can have bottles of milk or cartons of cream.
Here is part of the round-book.

Address	Milk	Cream	p
Westheath Road			
117	18	3	522
119	7	2	238
123	25	5	
125	11	1	
127	22	2	
133	7	2	
135	15	0	

The bill for 117 Westheath Road is 522p (or £5·22) and for
119 is £2·38. Kate's dad asks Kate to finish off the working out,
but Kate has forgotten the prices of a bottle of milk and a carton
of cream. However, when her dad gets back, Kate has filled in
all the amounts in the table.

See if you can work out the missing amounts yourself.

A4 The Megalopolitan Taxi Company charges all its drivers for diesel and oil supplied at the depot. The pump-attendant's record sheet looks like this.

Driver	Litres of diesel	Litres of oil	Cost in £
Ling	45	3	21
Instone	25	1	11
Harris	20	2	
Johnson	50	2	
Bibby	70	4	
Hersee	10	0	

(a) Calculate the amounts missing from the table.

(b) How much does 1 litre of diesel cost?

(c) How must does 1 litre of oil cost?

(d) Check that your answers for (b) and (c) give the correct costs for the first two drivers in the table.

A5 Megalopolis Council school meals service offers either hot meals or salads. There is a standard charge for a hot meal and a standard charge for a salad.

The estimated weekly needs of six schools are given in this table.

School	Hot meals	Salads	Income in £
Hightown	3000	1800	3900
Longridge	2400	1200	3000
Woodville	3600	1800	4000
Oakdene	2000	1200	2600
Lowfield	1200	600	1500
Leaway	1600	900	2050

(a) The estimated income has been worked out in a rush.
(The first two entries are correct.)
Can you spot any mistakes? Work out the correct figure for any mistake you find.

(b) Work out the charge for a hot meal.

(c) Work out the charge for a salad.

B Using letters

Here is another problem of the same type as those in section A.

In a pet shop, 2 frogs and 3 toads cost 60p;
3 frogs and 4 toads cost 87p.

We are not told the cost of a single frog or the cost of a single toad.
We can use letters to stand for these unknown costs.
Let a pence be the cost of one frog, and b pence be the cost of one toad.

The cost of 2 frogs is then $2a$ pence, and the cost of 3 toads is $3b$ pence.
So the first piece of information we are given can be 'translated' into an equation:

$$2a + 3b = 60$$

Similarly, the second piece of information becomes

$$3a + 4b = 87$$

We can use these two equations to find the cost of other collections of
frogs and toads. Here are some examples.

1 What is the cost of 4 frogs and 6 toads?

This is the same as finding the value of $4a + 6b$.

We get $4a + 6b$ by doubling $2a + 3b$. The working is set out like this:

$$2a + 3b = 60$$
Multiply both sides by 2. $2(2a + 3b) = 2 \times 60$
Remove brackets. $\mathbf{4a + 6b = 120}$

2 What is the cost of 5 frogs and 7 toads?

This is the same as finding the value of $5a + 7b$.

We get $5a + 7b$ by adding together $2a + 3b$ and $3a + 4b$.
The working is set out like this:

$$2a + 3b = 60$$
$$3a + 4b = 87$$
Add. $(2a + 3b) + (3a + 4b) = 60 + 87$

Put these brackets in. It will
help you to avoid mistakes later.

Remove brackets. $2a + 3b + 3a + 4b = 147$
Simplify. $5a + 7b = 147$

132

3 What is the cost of 1 frog and 1 toad?

This is the same as finding the value of $a + b$.

We get $a + b$ by subtracting $2a + 3b$ from $3a + 4b$, like this:

$$3a + 4b = 87$$
$$2a + 3b = 60$$

Subtract. $(3a + 4b) - (2a + 3b) = 87 - 60$

Remove brackets. $3a + 4b - 2a - 3b = 27$

Simplify. $a + b = 27$

In these three examples you can see three ways of using equations to get further equations. They are

(1) Multiplying both sides of an equation by the same number.

(2) Adding the left-hand sides of two equations and putting the result equal to the sum of the two right-hand sides.

(3) Subtracting the left-hand side of one equation from the left-hand side of the other, and putting the result equal to the difference of the two right-hand sides.

The purpose of questions B1 to B4 is to give you practice in working with equations.

B1 Start with these two equations: $a + 3b = 18$
$4a + 5b = 44$

From these equations, work out the value of each of the following expressions. In each case set out the working as shown in one of the three examples above.

(a) $2a + 6b$ (b) $5a + 8b$ (c) $3a + 2b$

B2 Start with these two equations: $2p + 5q = 67$
$3p + 7q = 83$

Work out the value of each of these expressions, showing working.

(a) $6p + 15q$ (b) $12p + 28q$ (c) $5p + 12q$ (d) $p + 2q$

B3 Start with these two equations: $9f + 5g = 77$
$6f + 3g = 48$

Which of the following are true? If you find a false one, give a correct version of it.

(a) $15f + 8g = 125$ (b) $90f + 50g = 770$ (c) $30f + 15g = 480$

(d) $3f + 2g = 19$ (e) $45f + 25g = 350$

B4 Start with these two equations: (1) $4a + 8b = 36$
                                         (2) $2a + 3b = 16$

(a) Use equation (2) to find the value of $4a + 6b$.

(b) Use equation (1) and the equation you got in part (a) to find the value of $2b$.

(c) From your answer to part (b) work out the value of b.

(d) Go back to equation (1). You know the value of b, so work out the value of a.

(e) Check that your values of a and b fit equation (2).

In questions B5 and B6 you are given information to translate into equations. From your equations you are asked to get further information.

B5 A gill is a liquid measure equal to one-quarter of a pint (in the south of England).
Spencer orders a pint of shandy made up of 2 gills of beer and 2 gills of lemonade. He pays 70p.
Helen pays 75p for a pint of shandy made up of 3 gills of beer and 1 gill of lemonade.

(a) Let x pence be the cost of 1 gill of beer, and
let y pence be the cost of 1 gill of lemonade.
Write down two equations, one for Spencer's shandy and one for Helen's.

(b) Use the first equation to find the value of $x + y$.

(c) Use the second equation and the equation you got in part (b) to find the value of $2x$.

(d) Write down the value of x.

(e) Work out the value of y.

(f) How much does a **pint** of beer cost?

(g) How much does a pint of lemonade cost?

B6 Gerda buys 7 ham rolls and 3 cheese rolls and pays 311p.
Connie buys 4 ham rolls and 1 cheese roll and pays 162p.

Let a pence be the cost of a ham roll and b pence the cost of a cheese roll.

(a) Write down two equations, one for Gerda's rolls and one for Connie's.

(b) Use one of the equations to get a new equation $12a + 3b = \ldots$

(c) Use this new equation and one of the original equations to find the value of $5a$. Then write down the value of a.

(d) Knowing the value of a, work out the value of b.

134

c Common solutions of two equations

Here are two equations: (1) $a + 3b = 17$
                        (2) $4a + 3b = 32$

If there is a pair of values of a and b which fits **both** equations, that pair is called a **common solution** of the two equations.

We can try to find a common solution by combining equations as we have been doing in section B.

By subtracting equation (1) from equation (2) we get

$$(4a + 3b) - (a + 3b) = 32 - 17$$
$$4a + 3b\ -\ a - 3b = 15$$
$$3a = 15$$
$$a = 5$$

Now we know that a is 5, we can find b from equation (1).

$$5 + 3b = 17$$
$$3b = 12$$
$$b = 4$$

> **C1**   Check that both of the equations $a + 3b = 17$ and $4a + 3b = 32$ are true when $a = 5$ and $b = 4$.

> **C2**   Find the common solution of the equations   (1) $5a + b = 25$
>   (2) $2a + b = 19$

> **C3**   Find the common solution of the equations   (1) $2a + b = 10$
>   (2) $2a + 5b = 22$

Suppose we want to find the common solution of   (1) $4a + b = 16$
                                                           (2) $a + 2b = 11$

When we subtract, we get this:
$$(4a + b) - (a + 2b) = 16 - 11$$
$$4a + b\ -\ a - 2b = 5$$
$$3a - b = 5$$

We are no better off than we were to begin with. Our equation still involves both a and b.

If we look back at the example at the top of this page we can see why subtraction worked there. When we subtracted we got

$$(4a + 3b) - (a + 3b) = 32 - 17$$
$$4a + 3b\ -\ a - 3b = 15$$

These cancel out.

By subtracting, we removed, or **eliminated**, one of the letters (b). This does not happen when the equations are $4a + b = 16$ and $a + 2b = 11$.

How can we get round this? Think about it before reading on.

We are trying to find the common solution of
(1) $4a + b = 16$
(2) $a + 2b = 11$

We would like to eliminate one of the letters, say b.
As we have $2b$ in the second equation we need to have $2b$ in the first as well. We can get this by multiplying both sides of equation (1) by 2.

$$2(4a + b) = 2 \times 16$$
$$8a + 2b = 32$$

Now we subtract equation (2) from this new equation, and b is eliminated.

$$(8a + 2b) - (a + 2b) = 32 - 11$$
$$8a + 2b - a - 2b = 21$$
$$7a = 21$$
$$a = 3$$

Knowing that a is 3, we can find the value of b from either equation (1) or (2). From equation (1), $(4 \times 3) + b = 16$, so $12 + b = 16$, so $b = 4$.

We can check that the values $a = 3$ and $b = 4$ do fit both equations:
(1) $4a + b = (4 \times 3) + 4 = 16$ ✓
(2) $a + 2b = 3 + (2 \times 4) = 11$ ✓
If you always do a check like this, you will always spot a wrong answer.

Instead of saying 'Find the common solution of . . .' we usually just say 'Solve . . .'.

C4 Solve the same pair of equations
(1) $4a + b = 16$
(2) $a + 2b = 11$
by eliminating a. (Multiply equation (2) by 4.)

C5 (a) Multiply both sides of the equation $p + 2q = 27$ by
(i) 2   (ii) 3   (iii) 4   (iv) 5

(b) Which of the results in part (a) would be useful in solving the pair of equations
(1) $p + 2q = 27$
(2) $3p + 5q = 71$
Solve these equations. Check that the common solution fits both equations.

C6 Solve each of the following pairs of equations in the way suggested.

(a) $7f + 3g = 19$ (Eliminate g.)
$2f + g = 6$

(b) $3r + 5s = 25$ (Eliminate r.)
$r + 4s = 13$

(c) $6a + 10b = 78$ (Eliminate either a or b.)
$3a + 2b = 30$

C7 Solve each of the following pairs of equations. Decide for yourself which letter to eliminate in each case.

(a) $2a + 3b = 13$
$4a + 5b = 25$

(b) $3h + 6k = 18$
$4h + 2k = 18$

(c) $5u + 2v = 21$
$10u + 8v = 54$

D Elimination by adding equations

So far we have eliminated a letter by subtracting one equation from another.
Sometimes we have to **add** two equations in order to eliminate a letter.
Here first is a simple example. Solve   (1) $3a + 2b = 25$
(2) $a - 2b = 3$

By adding the two equations, we get $(3a + 2b) + (a - 2b) = 25 + 3$
$$3a\boxed{+2b} + a\boxed{-2b} = 28$$

These cancel out. So b is eliminated.

$$4a = 28$$
$$a = 7$$

D1 (a) What equation do you get if you subtract equation (2) from equation (1)?
(b) Does this help you solve the equations?

D2 Solve each of these pairs of equations. Think whether you have to **add** or **subtract** the equations.

(a) $4a + 5b = 22$ (b) $2a - b = 8$ (c) $p + 3q = 10$
    $3a + 5b = 19$ $4a + b = 28$ $4p - 3q = 25$

The next example is not so straightforward.

Worked example

Solve the pair of equations   (1) $7a - 6b = 44$
(2) $3a + 2b = 28$

We notice that equation (1) has '$-6b$' and equation (2) has '$+2b$'.
If we multiply equation (2) by 3, we will get '$+6b$' in it.

Multiply equation (2) by 3: $3(3a + 2b) = 3 \times 28$
$$9a + 6b = 84$$

Add equation (1) to the new equation:

$$(7a - 6b) + (9a + 6b) = 44 + 84$$
$$7a - 6b + 9a + 6b = 128$$
$$16a = 128$$

$$a = \frac{128}{16} = 8$$

Go back to one of the original equations and put a equal to 8.
Equation (2) is slightly easier to do.

$$(3 \times 8) + 2b = 28$$
$$24 + 2b = 28$$
$$2b = 4$$
$$b = 2$$

D3 Solve the pair of equations (1) $4p - q = 13$
(2) $3p + 2q = 29$
by eliminating q. (Multiply equation (1) by 2.)

D4 Solve each of the following pairs of equations.
(a) $5s - 2t = 18$ (b) $6r + s = 13$ (c) $h + 3k = 15$
$3s + 4t = 16$ $5r - 4s = 6$ $5h - 9k = 3$

D5 Solve these pairs of equations.
(a) $2x + 3y = 23$ (b) $3x - 2y = 8$ (c) $2x + 5y = 37$
$5x + 6y = 50$ $5x + 8y = 70$ $6x + 3y = 27$

E Intersecting lines

This diagram shows the lines whose
equations are (1) $x + 2y = 10$
and (2) $x + y = 8$

The two lines intersect in a point A.

We can find the coordinates of the point of
intersection by drawing the two graphs.
But we can also **calculate** the coordinates
without doing any drawing.

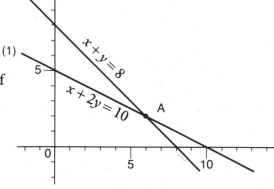

What do we mean when we say that the equation of line (1) is $x + 2y = 10$?

We mean that line (1) consists of all the points whose coordinates fit
the equation $x + 2y = 10$.

Similarly, line (2) consists of all the points whose coordinates fit the
equation $x + y = 8$.

The point of intersection, A, is on both lines. So the coordinates of A must
fit both equations together. In other words, the coordinates of A must be
the common solution of the two equations

(1) $x + 2y = 10$
(2) $x + y = 8$

By subtracting, we can find the value of y.

$$(x + 2y) - (x + y) = 10 - 8$$
$$x + 2y - x - y = 2$$
$$y = 2$$

Once we know y we can find x. From the fact $x + y = 8$, it follows
that $x = 6$. So the point of intersection of the two lines is the point (**6, 2**).

138

E1 The two lines whose equations are $3x + y = 9$ and $2x + y = 5$ intersect at a point.

Find the coordinates of the point of intersection by finding the common solution of the pair of equations.

E2 Find the coordinates of the point of intersection of the two lines $3x + 2y = 17$ and $4x + y = 21$. Check that the coordinates fit both equations.

E3 Find the coordinates of the point of intersection of each of these pairs of lines.

(a) $2x + 3y = 14$, $5x + 6y = 26$ (b) $3x - y = 20$, $4x + 2y = 30$

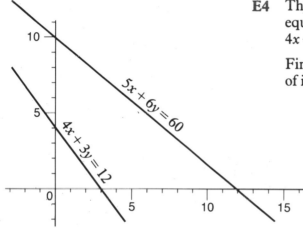

E4 This diagram shows the lines whose equations are $5x + 6y = 60$ and $4x + 3y = 12$.

Find the coordinates of their point of intersection.

E5 Find the coordinates of the point of intersection of each of these pairs of lines.

(a) $3x + 2y = 6$, $x - 2y = 10$ (b) $x + y = 4$, $3x + 2y = 5$

E6 If the three lines in this diagram are extended, they will make a triangle.

Find the coordinates of each of the three corners of the triangle.

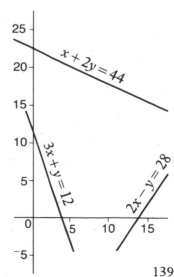

17 Distributions

A Percentiles

A firm making light bulbs tested a group of 500 bulbs to see
how long they lasted. 500 new bulbs were all switched on at the
same time, and the testers kept a record of how many of them had
'died' every so often afterwards. They produced their results in the
form of a graph.

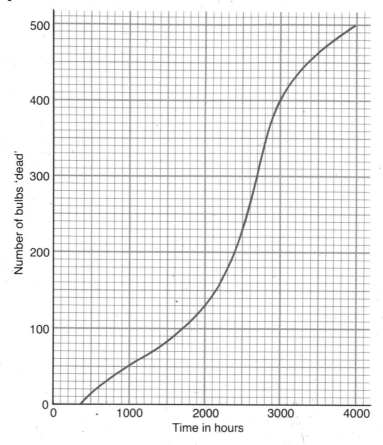

The graph shows, for example, that after 1000 hours 50 of the
bulbs were dead. After 4000 hours, all 500 bulbs were dead.

A1 (a) How many bulbs had lifetimes of 1000 hours or less?
    (b) How many had lifetimes of between 1000 and 2000 hours?
    (c) How many had lifetimes of between 2000 and 3000 hours?
    (d) After how many hours were 50% of the bulbs dead?
    (e) What was the shortest lifetime of a bulb?

The graph can easily be modified to show the **percentage** of the bulbs dead.

From the graph you can see that 40% of the bulbs had lifetimes of 2400 hours or less.

2400 hours is called the **40th percentile** of the bulbs' lifetimes.

The 40th percentile is the lifetime which splits the group of bulbs into 40% below it and 60% above.

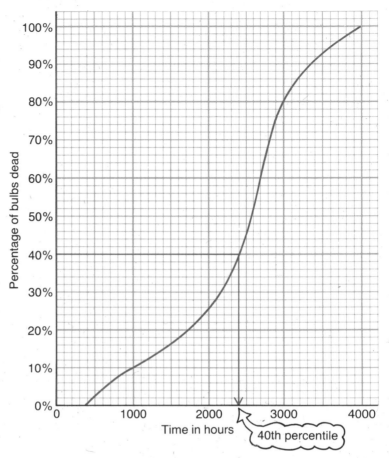

A2 Write down these percentiles of the bulbs' lifetimes.
(a) the 20th   (b) the 25th   (c) the 80th   (d) the 90th

A3 What percentile is   (a) 1500 hours   (b) 3200 hours

The 50th percentile is also called the **median**. The median of the bulbs' lifetimes is 2600 hours. (In other words, half of the bulbs lasted less than 2600 hours and half more than 2600 hours.)

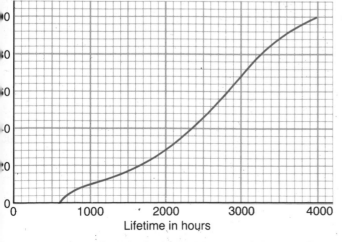

A4 This graph was obtained from a test on a different type of bulb. Write down

(a) the median lifetime

(b) the 60th percentile of the lifetimes

141

The 25th percentile is also called the **lower quartile**.
The 75th percentile is also called the **upper quartile**.

Between them, the quartiles and the median split the total number
of bulbs into four equal parts, like this.

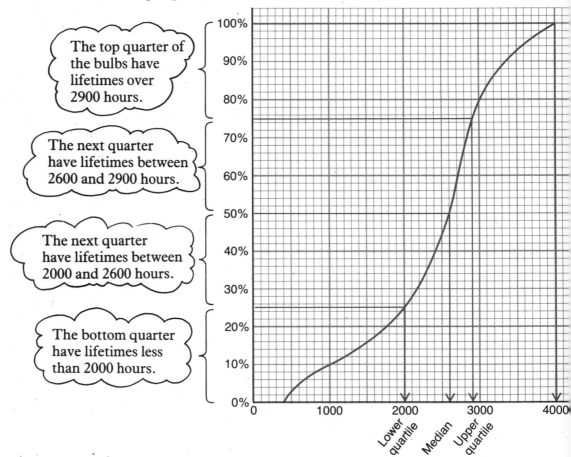

The top quarter of
the bulbs have
lifetimes over
2900 hours.

The next quarter
have lifetimes between
2600 and 2900 hours.

The next quarter
have lifetimes between
2000 and 2600 hours.

The bottom quarter
have lifetimes less
than 2000 hours.

The median and quartiles give useful information about how
the lifetimes of the bulbs are spread out or **distributed**.
Although the lifetimes in the group as a whole were spread out
between 400 hours (minimum) and 4000 hours (maximum), the
'middle half' of the group (the 2nd and 3rd quarters together)
were between 2000 and 2900 hours.

The information about the median and quartiles of a group of
measurements can be shown in the form of a 'box plot'.

The 'box' represents the middle
half of the group, whose lifetimes
are between the lower and upper
quartiles. The dotted line shows
the median. The 'tails' reach out
to the minimum and maximum
values.

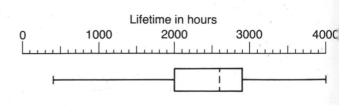

142

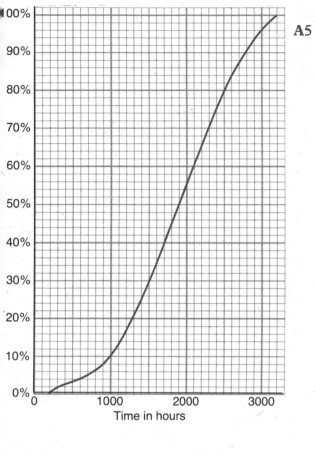

A5 This graph shows the results of testing a large sample of fluorescent tubes.

(a) What is the minimum lifetime?

(b) What is the lower quartile of the lifetimes?

(c) What is the median lifetime?

(d) What is the upper quartile of the lifetimes?

(e) What is the maximum lifetime?

(f) Draw a scale marked in hours (similar to the time axis of the graph). Beside the scale draw a 'box plot' of the distribution of the tubes' lifetimes.

Box plots are easier to draw if drawn on graph paper, something like this.

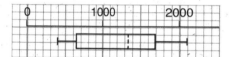

A6 A consumer guidance magazine tested large samples of two different makes of torch battery, to see how long they lasted. The graphs for the two brands, A and B, are shown here.

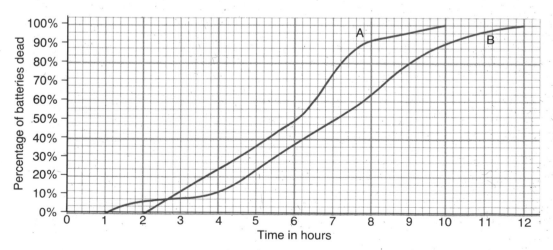

(a) Find the minimum, maximum, median and quartiles of the lifetimes of each brand.

(b) Draw two box plots side by side to compare the distributions.

(c) Which brand appears to be better?

B Cumulative frequency

The weights, in grams, of some potatoes are marked on this scale.

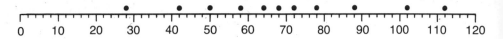

Imagine you are moving a pointer along the scale, starting at the lower end. As you move along the scale you count the potatoes.

There are no potatoes at all until you reach 28 g. Then the number goes up from 0 to 1. At 42 g the number goes up from 1 to 2, and so on.

We can draw a graph to show how the counting goes.

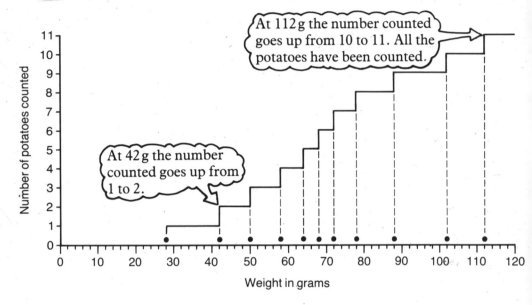

At 112 g the number counted goes up from 10 to 11. All the potatoes have been counted.

At 42 g the number counted goes up from 1 to 2.

If there is a large number of potatoes the graph could look like this. (The steps are not so high because the scale on the vertical axis is different.)

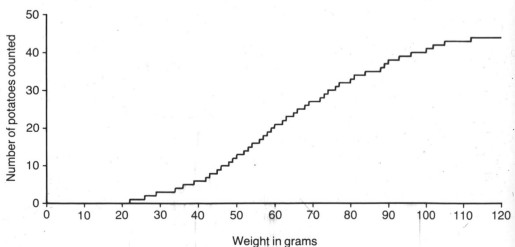

These graphs are called **cumulative frequency graphs**.

With an even larger collection of potatoes, the cumulative frequency graph would be indistinguishable from a curve, as in this example.

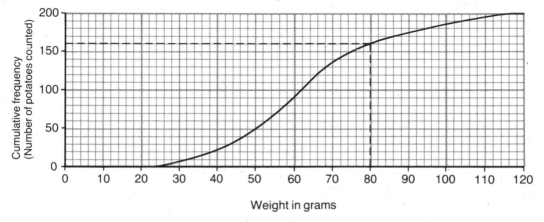

It is important to know what a cumulative frequency graph tells you.

Imagine you are moving a pointer along the 'weight' scale of the graph above.
There are no potatoes at all until you reach 24 g.
As you move along from 24 g, so you count more and more potatoes.

For example, by the time you reach 80 g you have counted 160 potatoes.
This is shown by the dotted lines on the graph.
In other words **160 potatoes weigh 80 g or less**.

Moving on further, by the time you reach 116 g you have counted all of the potatoes (200 in all). The graph flattens out after this.
So 116 g is the maximum weight.

B1 (a) How many of the potatoes shown on the graph above weigh 60 g or less?

(b) How many weigh 70 g or less?

(c) How many weigh 100 g or less?

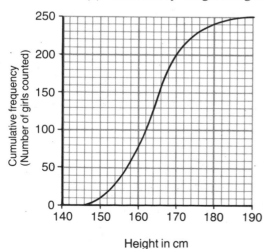

B2 This cumulative frequency graph is based on the heights of 250 girls aged 15.

(a) How many of the girls have heights of 170 cm or less?

(b) How many have heights of 160 cm or less?

(c) So how many have heights between 160 cm and 170 cm?

145

The graphs given in section A (showing the lifetimes of light bulbs) are also cumulative frequency graphs.

We can replace the vertical scale (cumulative frequency, or number counted) by a percentage scale (cumulative percentage).

The graph below gives information about the weights of tomatoes in a large sample.

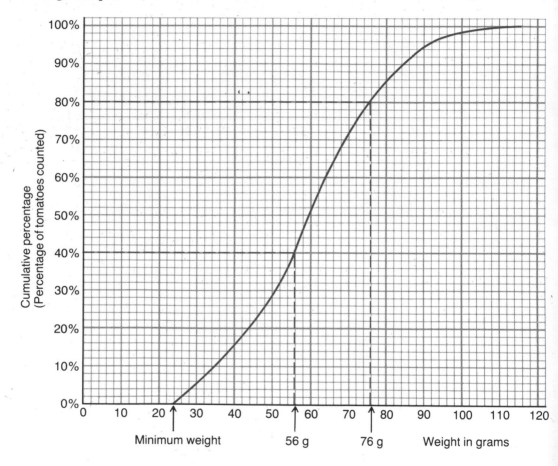

B3 (a) What percentage of the tomatoes weigh 44 g or less?

(b) What percentage weigh 90 g or less?

56 grams is the **40th percentile** of the tomatoes' weights. 40% of them weigh 56 g or less.

76 grams is the **80th percentile**.

As before, the 25th percentile is called the **lower quartile**, the 50th the **median**, and the 75th the **upper quartile**.

B4 (a) Find the values of the lower quartile, median and upper quartile of the tomatoes' weights.

(b) Draw a scale of weight in grams and a box plot to show the distribution of the tomatoes' weights.

B5 This graph is based on the waist measurements of a group of 15-year-old girls.

Find the lower quartile, median and upper quartile of the waist measurements.

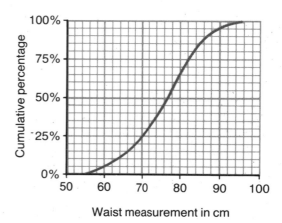

Waist measurement in cm

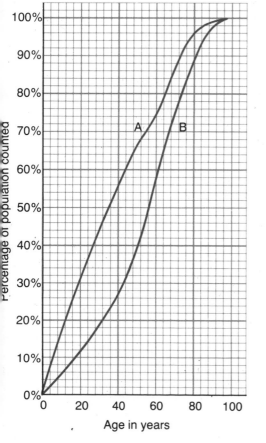

Age in years

B6 These graphs illustrate the distribution of ages in the populations of two towns A and B.

(a) Complete these sentences.

(i) Half of the population of town A are below the age of . . .

(ii) Half of the population of town B are below the age of . . .

(iii) . . .% of the population of town A are 80 or over.

(iv) . . .% of the population of town B are 80 or over.

(b) One of the towns is a new town with housing estates and many factories. The other is a seaside town which attracts retired people. Which town is which?

(c) Find from the graph the lower and upper quartiles of the age of the population in town A.

(d) Do the same for town B.

(e) If you split the population of town B into age-groups 0–10, 10–20, 20–30, and so on, which group would contain the largest number of people?

147

C The inter-quartile range

Here are box plots of the age distributions in the two towns A and B.

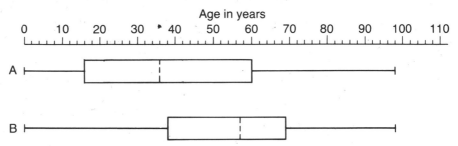

You can see from these that the overall range of the ages in the two towns is the same (0 to 98, i.e. 98 years). But in town A the 'middle half' of the population is spread out between 16 years and 60 years, while in town B the 'middle half' is spread out between 38 and 69.

The range of the 'middle half', between the lower quartile and the upper quartile, is often used as a way of comparing the spread of two populations. The overall range is not much use, because there are always likely to be one or two very young or very old people in the population. The overall range can give a very misleading idea of the spread of the population as a whole.

The difference between the upper and lower quartiles is called the **inter-quartile range**. It is shown by the length of the 'box'.

For town A, the inter-quartile range is $60-16 = 44$ years.
For town B, the inter-quartile range is $69-38 = 31$ years.

By comparing inter-quartile ranges we see that the ages of the population of town A are generally more spread out than those of town B.

C1 Find the inter-quartile range of the weights of the tomatoes illustrated in the graph on page 146.

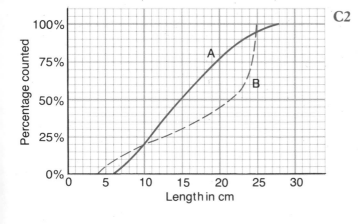

C2 This graph illustrates the distribution of lengths in two populations of worms

(a) Find the median and quartiles of the lengths in each population.

(b) Draw two box plots, one for each population.

(c) Work out the inter-quartile range for each population.

(d) In which population are the length more widely spread out on the whole?

D Frequency and cumulative frequency

Here again is the graph from page 140, showing the results of testing a sample of light bulbs.

The vertical axis shows the actual number of bulbs dead, not the percentage.

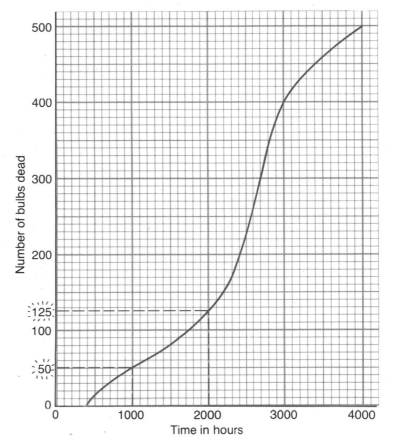

It is quite easy to find from the graph the number of bulbs with lifetimes from 0 to 1000 hours, 1000 to 2000 hours, and so on.

There are 50 bulbs in the 0–1000 hours group.
There are 125 in the 0–2000 hours group, so the number in the 1000–2000 hours group must be 125−50 = 75.

D1 Copy and complete this table, using the information given in the graph.

Lifetime in hours	Frequency (number of bulbs)
0–1000	50
1000–2000	75
2000–3000	
3000–4000	
Total	_____

Now suppose the problem is the other way round: how can you draw a graph like the one above when you are given the information in the frequency table?

Here is the completed frequency table for question D1.

The problem is how to draw a cumulative frequency graph from the information given in this table.

Lifetime in hours	Frequency
0 – 1000	50
1000 – 2000	75
2000 – 3000	275
3000 – 4000	100
Total	500

To make the explanation easier to follow, here first is an ordinary frequency chart.

Think about a pointer moving along the horizontal scale.

By the time you reach 1000 hours, you have counted 50 bulbs.

By the time you reach 2000 hours, you have counted an extra 75 bulbs, making 125 so far. And so on.

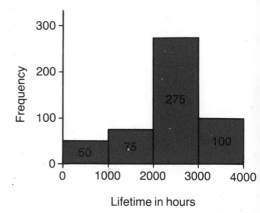

So we can make a **cumulative frequency table** from the ordinary frequency table, like this.

Frequency table

Lifetime in hours	Frequency
0–1000	50
1000–2000	75
2000–3000	275
3000–4000	100

Cumulative frequency table

Lifetime in hours	Cumulative frequency
up to 1000	50
up to 2000	125
up to 3000	400
up to 4000	500

Add together the '0–1000' and '1000–2000' groups.

Add on the '2000–3000' group.

Add on the '3000–4000' group.

From the cumulative frequency table we can plot four points on the cumulative frequency graph.

The rest of the graph has to be largely guesswork, but it can be used to find rough estimates of percentiles (including the median and quartiles).

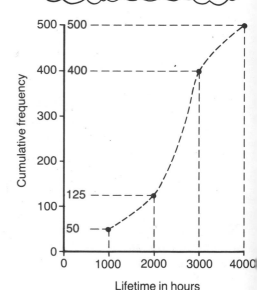

D2 A sample of 400 potatoes were weighed and sorted into groups with weights 0–20 g, 20–40 g, and so on.

Here is the frequency table.

Weight in grams	Frequency
0–20	23
20–40	74
40–60	126
60–80	104
80–100	62
100–120	11

(a) Copy and complete this cumulative frequency table.

(b) Draw a cumulative frequency graph and use it to estimate the median weight of the sample.

Weight in grams	Cumulative frequency
up to 20	23
up to 40	97
up to 60	223

D3 This frequency table gives information about the weekly earnings of the employees in a firm.

(a) Make a cumulative frequency table. The left-hand column will go 'up to 50, up to 60, up to 80', and so on.

(b) Draw a cumulative frequency graph and estimate the median weekly earnings.

Earnings in £	Number of employees
0–50	38
50–60	230
60–80	21
80–100	17
100–150	3
150–200	27
200–250	14
	Total 350

D4 (a) Use the method of 'mid-interval values' to estimate the mean of the weekly earnings from the table in question D3. (Make a table like the one below.)

Earnings in £	Mid-interval value, £	Number of employees	Contribution to total, in £
0–50	25	38	950
50–60	55	230	12650
		and so on	
Totals		_____	_____

(b) Which value, the mean or the median, gives a better idea of the 'average' level of earnings in the firm?

14 Volume

14.1 Calculate the volume of the triangular prism shown in this diagram. All measurements are in cm.

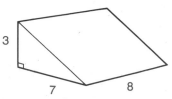

14.2 A swimming pool whose area is $96 \, m^2$ contains $170 \, m^3$ of water. The depth of the water is the same everywhere. Calculate the depth of the water, to the nearest cm.

14.3 A copper disc has a radius of $3 \cdot 5 \, cm$ and a thickness of $0 \cdot 2 \, cm$. Calculate

(a) its volume

(b) its mass, given that the density of copper is $8 \cdot 9 \, g/cm^3$

14.4 (a) Calculate the volume of a cylinder whose radius is $6 \cdot 65 \, m$ and whose height is $7 \cdot 20 \, m$, to the nearest m^3.

(b) Write down the volume of a cylinder with

(i) the same radius but twice the height

(ii) the same height but twice the radius

14.5 A solid steel column has a circumference of $4 \cdot 45 \, m$ and is $3 \cdot 60 \, m$ tall.

(a) Calculate the radius of the cross-section of the column.

(b) Calculate the volume of the column.

14.6

(a) Calculate the volume of the wine in this full glass.

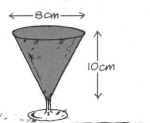

(b) This is the same glass, but the wine is now only half as deep. Calculate the volume of wine.

(c) How much wine will there be in the glass if it is filled to $\frac{3}{4}$ of its maximum depth?

15 Problems in planning

15.1 Four clerks work in an office. Each one is entitled to 3 weeks holiday, but not more than 2 weeks can be taken in any one stretch.
They all have to take their holidays within a period of 6 weeks, but not more than two of the clerks are allowed to be away at the same time.

(a) Make a holidays timetable for them.
(b) Explain why it would be impossible to squeeze all their holidays into a 5-week period.

15.2 A company has decided to build new offices on a plot of land which it owns, and a list of the necessary activities has been drawn up by the building contractor. These activities are given in the table below.

Activity	Description	Preceding activities	Time taken (in weeks)
A	Draw up plans	—	3
B	Order furniture and office equipment	A	1
C	Level the site	A	3
D	Mark out site	C	2
E	Lay drainage	D and B	4
F	Make approach roads	D and B	3
G	Lay foundations	E	7
H	Erect walls	G	12
I	Lay paths	F and H	4
J	Erect roof	H	2
K	Erect internal walls	J	5
L	Complete building	K	10

Find out the shortest time in which the new offices can be built.
You may find it helpful to draw some kind of diagram.
(This question is based on a question set by the Institute of Chartered Secretaries and Administrators.)

16 Linear equations

16.1 Solve each of these pairs of equations. Check each solution.

(a) $4a - b = 3$
$3a + b = 11$

(b) $5p + 2q = 32$
$3p + q = 19$

(c) $7s - 3t = 16$
$5s + 6t = 44$

16.2 The lines whose equations are $x + 2y = 14$ and $3x + 2y = 19$ intersect at the point A. Find the coordinates of A.

16.3 Christmas wine-baskets are made up of seven bottles as follows.

Pack	Gutrotwein von Deutschland	Suave Vino Bianco d'Italia	Price
A	2 bottles	5 bottles	£13·70
B	4 bottles	3 bottles	£14·10

(a) Choose letters to stand for the cost of 1 bottle of Gutrotwein and for the cost of 1 bottle of Suave. Write down your letters and what they stand for.

(b) Write down an equation based on the cost of pack A, and another based on the cost of pack B.

(c) Solve the equations to find the cost of 1 bottle of each wine.

16.4 Find the coordinates of the point of intersection of each of the following pairs of lines.

(a) $5x + y = 17$
    $3x + 2y = 6$

(b) $3x - 2y = 18$
    $2x + y = 19$

(c) $4x - y = 9$
    $7x + 3y = 13$

17 Distributions

17.1 A football match started at 2:30 p.m. but the gates of the football ground opened at 1:30 p.m.
This graph shows how the number of people inside the ground grew between 1 p.m. and 3 p.m.

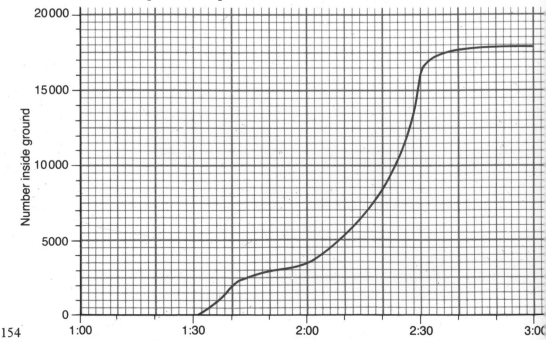

(a) How many people came to the match?
(b) How many arrived after the match had started?
(c) What was the median arrival time (the time by which half of the total number had arrived)?
(d) What were the lower and upper quartiles of the arrival times?

17.2 Saturday shoppers in two towns A and B were asked how far they had travelled to get to the shops. The results are shown in these cumulative frequency graphs.

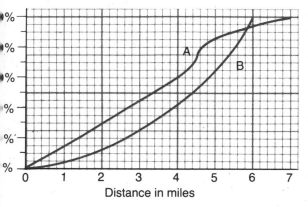

Distance in miles

(a) What was the median of the distances travelled by shoppers in each town?

(b) Draw two 'box plots' alongside each other to show the distributions of travelling distances in the towns.

(c) In which town do shoppers travel further on the whole to get to the shops?

17.3 This frequency table gives information about the heights of the trees in an area of forest.

Height in metres	10–15	15–20	20–25	25–30	30–35	35–40
Frequency	19	28	34	30	13	3

(a) Make a cumulative frequency table.
(b) Draw a cumulative frequency graph.
(c) Use the graph to estimate the median height of the trees.

M Miscellaneous

M1 This diagram shows a regular pentagon whose sides are each 6 cm long.

(a) Calculate the angle marked c.

(b) Calculate the length marked h. (A right-angled triangle has been picked out to help you.)

(c) Calculate the area of the pentagon, to the nearest $0 \cdot 1 \, \text{cm}^2$.

(d) What will be the area of a regular pentagon whose sides are each (i) 12 cm long (ii) 18 cm long

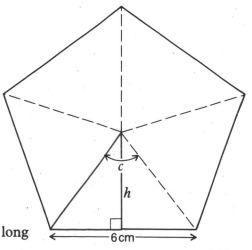

6 cm

M2 Solve each of these equations. Give each answer to 1 d.p.

(a) $15 \cdot 8 - 4 \cdot 5x = 9 \cdot 7$ (b) $\dfrac{x}{0 \cdot 8} - 13 \cdot 5 = 47 \cdot 1$ (c) $\dfrac{0 \cdot 9}{x} = 3 \cdot 4$

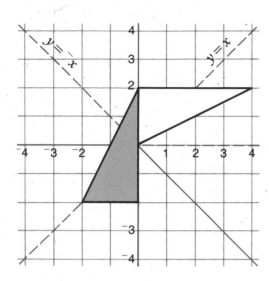

M3 The white triangle in this diagram is to be mapped onto the grey triangle by using a pair of mappings.

Describe the mapping which is missing in each of these pairs.

(a) Reflection in the x-axis, followed by . . .

(b) Rotation 180° about (0, 0), followed by . . .

(c) Translation with vector $\begin{bmatrix} -2 \\ -2 \end{bmatrix}$, followed by . . .

(d) Rotation 90° anticlockwise about (2, 0), followed by . . .

M4 I have five cards: 2 jacks, a queen, a king and an ace.
I shuffle the cards and a friend takes two at random.

(a) Make a list of all the possible pairs of cards which she could have chosen.

(b) What is the probability that she picks the two jacks?

M5 The mean weight of n pigs is p kg.

(a) Write an expression for the total weight of the pigs.
(b) An extra pig weighing q kg is added to the group.
Write an expression for the new mean weight.

M6 This is the menu at a roadside café.
Work out the cost of each individual item (sausage, egg, bacon, chips).
Explain how you did it.

Menu

Sausage, egg & chips	7c
Bacon, egg & chips	7s
Sausage, bacon & chips	84
Sausage, bacon & egg	5ε

M7 Monty has some rabbits and some hutches.
If one rabbit goes in each hutch there is one rabbit left over.
If two rabbits go into each hutch there is one hutch left over.

How many rabbits are there and how many hutches?